Aggro

The Illusion of
Violence

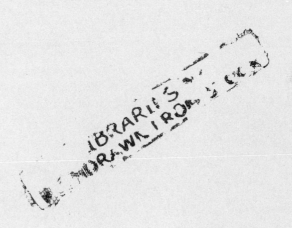

Aggro

The Illusion of Violence

Peter Marsh

With a foreword by
DESMOND MORRIS

J. M. Dent & Sons Ltd
London, Melbourne and Toronto

First published 1978
© Peter Marsh 1978

Printed in Great Britain by
Biddles Ltd, Guildford, Surrey
and bound at the
Aldine Press, Letchworth, Herts
for
J. M. Dent & Sons Ltd,
Aldine House, Albemarle Street, London

This book is set in VIP 10 on 11pt Times

British Library Cataloguing in Publication Data
Marsh, Peter
　Aggroman.
　1. Aggressiveness (Psychology)
　I. Title
　301.6'33　　　　BF575.A3

ISBN 0-460-12026-3

Contents

Foreword by Desmond Morris

Late one night, back in 1957, my wife and I had just completed a script for a television programme I was presenting the next day. We had skipped dinner and, suddenly realizing how hungry we were, we set off at midnight to look for a restaurant. The nearest one we found was a scruffy cafe with peeling paint in Camden Town, but we were so tired that we searched no further. As we entered, I regretted our decision, because there, at a long table near the counter, sat the only other customers, a noisy gang of savage-looking young Teddy Boys, two of whom were studiously paring their finger-nails with long, glinting flick-knives. Selecting a table as far away as possible, we ordered our meal and started to eat it as unobtrusively as we could. The gang were peering at us and whispering among themselves, as if plotting some strategy, and I realized that my palms were beginning to sweat. The sweating increased when, as one of them got up to pay the man behind the counter, the rest swaggered across and surrounded our table. They muttered something like 'we're taking care of you and your missus' and left. I could hear them talking outside and was convinced that, when we too left, we were in for serious trouble. 'Multiple stab wounds' and 'brutal gang rape' were the phrases that flitted insistently through my mind, as I finally went up to settle our bill. To my astonishment, I was told that our meal had already been paid for by the flick-knife boys. 'They said they'd taken care of your bill, didn't they?' Outside on the pavement they were waiting, not to plunge in a sharp-pointed blade, but to wish us goodnight and to tell us that last week's TV programme 'wasn't half bad'.

This little incident taught me a lesson that, as a student of animal aggression, I should have known – namely, that for all animals, including the human animal, aggressive displays rarely lead to bloodshed. The gang of Teddy Boys had effectively dominated their territory – their local cafe – and that was satisfaction enough. They had not only seen me subdued and apprehensive in their apparently

7

threatening presence, but they had also been able to display their social control neatly in a second way, by taking charge of our bill. Although this was a friendly act in response to seeing me on TV, it also, at the same time, gave them the subtle dominance that a host has over his guests, and was a further way of displaying their status on their home ground.

Peter Marsh would not be surprised by this story, because unlike the dismal hordes of armchair experts who scribble endlessly on the subject of human aggression without ever truly studying it, he has gone out into the real world as a painstaking observer and an honest reporter of what he sees there. He belongs to a new breed of psychologist, a breed that is increasingly abandoning the ivory tower of the sterile laboratory and going 'where the action is'. His book is full of objective descriptions of what actually happens when human beings confront one another and display their rivalries. He succinctly cuts through the web of abstract theorizing and ideologically warped preaching about what people should and should not do, and spells out the truth about 'aggro' as it really is. He will upset many people who have pontificated on the subject, if only because he refuses to follow the easy, fashionable lines of argument, which condemn out of hand all forms of human aggression without ever stopping to examine the true function of this common form of behaviour.

It is hard to praise him too highly for what he has written, and if the importance of his message goes unheeded, then as a society we will be the poorer. Before reading his words, try to forget all you have seen in the media on the topic of 'savage thugs'. Try to view the subject as if you are encountering it for the first time. He is in no way condoning violence, and if you feel that, you will be grossly misreading him. But he *is* trying to put the aggressive behaviour of our species into a true perspective and to transmit to us a timely warning against hysterical reactions and panic predictions that, if unchecked, may well carry the seeds of their own fulfilment. Make no mistake, this is an important book.

Oxford 1978

Acknowledgments

To acknowledge fully all the help and assistance provided by friends and colleagues during the preparation of this book is a difficult task. Sometimes a chance remark or argument can lead to a radical reshaping of ideas and research work long after the situation out of which such change emerged is forgotten. Some individuals, however, must be singled out.

A special debt is owed to Robin Fox who, when he gave a seminar in Oxford some years ago concerning fights among rural Irishmen, gave me confidence and confirmed a sense of direction in the quest to understand everyday violence and aggression.

A similar debt is owed to Desmond Morris who has provided, over the last few years, unstinting support and encouragement and a continuous supply of good ideas.

Thanks also to the following for many different things: Christine Adcock, Michael Argyle, Rad Babic, Michael Brenner, Marylin Brenner, Anne Campbell, Peter Collett, Jerry Ginsburg, Peter Hancock, Rom Harré, Roger Ingham, Chris Lightbown, Peter McPhail, Steven Muncer, Marie O'Shaughnessy, Chris Riley, John Tagholm.

Ann McKendry produced typewritten order out of pieces of pencilled manuscript and dictation.

Finally, special thanks to Tricia Marsh who put up with it all even though she had doubts.

Peter Marsh
Oxford, 1978

Introduction

Our current fascination with violence is almost unique. It is matched only by the Victorians' fervent concern with sex. We protest an abhorrence of fights, injury and murder, yet we manufacture more images of violence, in the name of news and entertainment, than of any other facet of human behaviour. From reading the breakfast newspaper to switching off the late-night movie we become more and more convinced that our societies are reaching new peaks in the business of chaotic self-destruction. We are outraged and appalled. But we are also 'vicariously aroused. For when the effects are indirect, violence is fun.

This ambivalence, in itself, is not new. Children have always laughed at the Punch and Judy show and men have travelled many miles to see a public execution or a good flogging. Our modern intoxication, however, has seriously changed the extent to which we are able to distinguish between different types of violence. In the current hysterical excitement, events like mugging, dance-hall brawls, child battering, football hooliganism and school-playground fights all merge into a single murky but magnetic category. We are far less able to see that some events present only an illusion of violence, whilst others threaten our continued survival.

In failing to make these distinctions we present ourselves with enormous problems. Because we don't understand aggression, and because we fail to realize that it might have a variety of consequences – some of which can be socially useful – we find it increasingly difficult to manage the process. And, by failing to see that 'aggro' – the kind of aggressive activity which crops up in stylized 'bundles' outside dance-halls, in Punk Rock clubs and on the football terraces – is special, we begin to change the whole pattern of violence within our communities.

'Aggro' is a way of expressing aggression in a relatively non-injurious manner. Football 'hooligans', despite all the mythologies about them which circulate in the media, are currently the most

11

visible exponents in Britain of this ritualistic mode of conflict resolution. They, however, have had many predecessors in history and their patterns of social behaviour have equivalents in many other countries. Their rituals also have much in common with those associated with tribal warfare in less developed societies. Furthermore, virtually all other species of animal appear to have behaviour patterns which, at one level, are strikingly similar.

Generations before us have lived with these rituals and have understood their social utility. They have been able to make the distinctions which are now clouded over in the wake of fear and outrage. Modern society calls for scapegoats – for identifiable demons to be held responsible for all our failings. But in a world of nuclear overkill, terrorism and increasing alienation, we pick strange targets. We pick Punks and Teddy Boys and soccer fans and we lose our grip on rational perception and understanding.

As we appear to become more murderous, we look for easy explanations. We seize upon notions of instinct – a scientifically disguised version of the 'original sin' doctrine. Or we blame the environment, lack of parental discipline or poor schools. But we miss the point. By trying to eradicate aggro we end up with something far more sinister. Instead of social violence we get non-social violence which manifests itself in random, gratuitous injury. We wish that aggression would go away and we invent fanciful ideas of peaceful Utopias.

But aggression doesn't go away, and the champions of pacifist ideals have never had history on their side. It remains and it demands social management. Our patterns of violence don't reflect our inherent propensity towards butchery. They reflect our successes and our failures in the business of conflict management. And it is with the nature of such failures and with the opportunities for success that we must be concerned.

'A little bit of violence never hurt anyone'

Graffiti in London

Aggro

'Aggro' is a term which is peculiarly British. It is rarely used in other English-speaking countries, with the possible exception of Australia, and in America, in particular, it seems to be virtually unknown. But 'aggro' has interesting origins. It started life in the early 1960s, mainly in the graffiti daubed on the walls and fences of faceless housing estates in London. It was particularly associated with Skinheads and the emerging generation of rather special football supporters – the fans who later became stuck with the catch-all label of hooligans. In those days aggro was 'agro', and it was not until journalists and social commentators got hold of the term that it was modified to accord with the normal English language conventions for matching pronunciations and spelling. Despite this attempt by the establishment to take over the word the old form still exists. It crops up most noticeably in some of the chants which are regularly heard at football matches. For example:

A-G; A-G-R; A-G-R-O; AGRO.

In everyday social talk, aggro figures prominently as a means of referring to conflict and the resolution of conflict. It expresses aggravation – in fact, this is the root of the term. It also sums up an aggressive determination to do something about the state of affairs. The source of the conflict may often seem rather trivial, almost manufactured out of thin air. The extent of the felt aggravation may also be fairly small. But men and young boys fight, as they have always fought, in the streets, in schools, in dance halls, pubs or sports grounds. And although the word aggro may be of recent origin, it captures something which is as old as man himself. For its most distinguishing features are the style and the ceremonies through which conflicts are resolved. The 'fights' are special. The displays of hostility, the issuing of threats and the conventions of challenge and counter-challenge make up a distinctive and important part of man's social means of coping with the problems of

13

attackers flee from the pursuing police, the victim slowly gets up, rubs himself a bit and then he too runs off to avoid arrest. There is something remarkable about this piece of film. At first sight it looked as if someone was being seriously injured. A rain of boots to the body is not something to be taken lightly. But when we look more closely we see that although the attackers perform kicking movements which are savagely exaggerated, the boot itself often stops short of the body – it digs into the turf near the victim's head, and he is rarely subjected to the full, and potentially fatal, impact of an unconstrained blow. It is almost as if this were a real movie, with the fans as extras ordered to play out a scene of violence for the benefit of the cameras. They put on a show that is convincing. We are fooled by it.

Nobody is going to suggest that in situations like this people never get hurt. Even on the film set actors and stunt-men sometimes misjudge things. In acting out fight scenes members of the cast will occasionally deliver a real blow that causes damage. The contrast is not between total injury and complete safety but rather between what would happen if there were no constraints, and what happens in reality.

The analogy between football fans and actors is a useful one for our purposes, but we should not run away with the idea that these young people are playing out their scenes in an intentional way. In fact, if you casually asked a fan what was going on in the clip of film he would probably use words like 'riot', or 'a good kicking' and suggest that the fans on the pitch were, indeed, 'putting the boot in'. No – aggro is restrained violence, but this restraint is not usually something which is deliberate or planned.

The scenario is not a typical one in the sense that such events mark the extremes of violence in such situations. The commentary is real enough though and comes, in fact, from the BBC's reporting of an end of season match between Manchester United and Manchester City. The match was abandoned because of a 'pitch invasion'. It was also the season which saw United relegated to the second division. A lot was at stake in this match, and when the stakes are high even the strongest of informal constraints can lose some of their effectiveness. But even at times like these the system doesn't break down completely and there is still an element of order remaining which is sufficient to prevent a catastrophe. For a fully representative case we have to follow groups of football fans and observe the wholly predictable features of the event which marks the high point of their week. A few years ago we might have followed the Mods and Rockers as they sped down the South Coast

16

to battle it out on the beaches of Clacton and Brighton. Before that we could have hung around the Teddy Boys outside the dance-hall to wait for the big 'bundle'. Two thousand years ago we might have witnessed the rampaging mob leaving the amphitheatre at Pompeii.

'Football' begins early on Saturdays. When there is an away match the enthusiastic fan might have to get up at the crack of dawn to travel hundreds of miles. But at least the distances in Britain are such that it is possible, with determination and some expense, to get to where your team is playing. In the USA and other countries this is just not possible – which may account to some extent for the lack of fan-aggro in America. You can't have a pitched battle in New York with fans from Los Angeles, whatever the sport. They all stay at home and watch it on TV. Since the mid 1960s in Britain, however, teenagers, with their increasing affluence, have been able to afford the cost of chartered trains and coaches to take them to where the action is.

Even for home games the day starts early. Aggro isn't, nor has it ever been, just about fighting. It has been to do with this distinct ceremony – a ceremony we associate with the tournaments in the Middle Ages or the elaborate spectacles of the Roman and Byzantine eras. Football fans may be less sophisticated in their style of dress, but they have evolved highly distinctive costumes; their 'gear'. There are symbols of allegiance to be donned along with clothes which communicate images of strength, masculinity and loyalty. This image building can be taken to extremes. In the depths of winter and in sub-zero temperatures you can often see young lads wearing only thin shirts and jeans. Some wear no shirts at all and are determined to let rivals view their toughness. But they always wear boots.

An important element of aggro is bluff, and boots and bare chests are very much part of this act. In its purest form, in fact, aggro is the art of subduing one's rival simply by conning him into thinking that his cause is lost from the outset. The aim is to achieve the end that a violent assault might but without resorting to violence (in a serious sense) at all. We can see this particular gambit enacted every Saturday in and around soccer games but it goes on everywhere. It is so common that we rarely pay any attention to it. Consider this second, and extremely typical, scenario and think back to the school playground or the street corner of your childhood.

The scene is a tea-stall and the surrounding concourse during half-time at a football game. Rival groups of supporters, having been carefully separated from each other during the game by fences and a cordon of policemen, have a chance to 'get-at' some of the opposition on these occasions. Rarely, however, do the two groups tear headlong into each other. Instead the confrontations are much more subtle. The leading fans of each team take up defiant postures at a distance of some twenty feet or so apart. Some lean against a wall, one leg crossed in front of the other and hands in pockets. Others stand with one hand on hip, looking sideways, not face-on, at their enemies. Police mingle in between the two groups adopting somewhat wary expressions and affecting an air of calm indifference.

In a corner of the concourse a small drama starts up. A few fans from the away team sit on the steps drinking tea. Some local lads cautiously approach them in a manner which cuts off their contact with the main body of their mates. Their retreat is prevented by a wall behind them – they are literally cornered. The home fans begin to issue stereotyped insults and veiled challenges. There's a very special kind of body movement which accompanies the verbal abuse. The torso swivels above the hips, shoulders are pulled back, fists are clenched and the head raised and turned slightly to one side. It's the standard male 'swagger' – a piece of characteristic signalling which crops up whenever groups of men and lads are out to impress their peers and destroy the confidence of their rivals. Although these away fans are only slightly outnumbered they make no response. They are on foreign territory. It's not their patch and they have learned that tolerance of a certain level of provocation in these circumstances is very judicious. A policeman watches out of the corner of his eye.

A member of the home group moves forward to lead the antagonism and singles out one of the visitors as his target victim. He approaches very close to him and begins to flick his jacket collar, maintaining a barrage of imprecations and threats which have suddenly become much more explicit. The victim reddens and looks fixedly at the ground in front of him. Eventually provoked beyond endurance, he looks at his assailant. Immediately he is accused of staring: 'Who do you think you're screwing you cunt?' The victim now has no choice. He must respond. He jumps up and one pace backwards from his rival and takes up a stance which indicates a willingness to fight. It's the 'come-on-then' posture – feet apart, arms outstretched, hands at hip level. The two protagonists stand facing each other, staring cautiously and waiting for the other to move. The other fans have nervously moved back a pace or two – partly to get out of the way and partly to prevent others (including the police) disrupting the 'fight'. For what seems a very long time, nothing happens. There is extreme tension in the air but no one throws a punch. The fighters shuffle a bit as if waiting for divine intervention. Such intervention finally arrives in the form of a much older fan who grabs the arm of his younger colleague and pulls him aside. The visiting victim is surrounded by his own group and the scene begins to break up. The policeman who has remained at some distance from this event moves forward and urges everybody to clear away, which they do. The episode has taken twelve minutes.

This apparently inconsequential vignette may seem quite unremarkable and yet it highlights many of the important processes which constitute contemporary aggro. Beneath the surface of these confrontations many social mechanisms are at work and it is through attention to these that we begin to make some progress in understanding what are often taken to be senseless and pointless patterns of behaviour. Let's examine the actual sequence of actions in the tea-stall example more closely.

One of the major features of such conflicts is the interplay of recognized symbols. Symbols are essential for the recognition of conflict in a manner which is orderly and 'safe'. They serve, in fact, in place of forceful combat and can be isolated in streams of activity which, on the surface, appear chaotic. Such symbols are to be found at two levels. Firstly, there are those which are common to virtually all conflict situations, not only between people but also between animals. Secondly, there are symbols which are effective only within a particular social context or micro-culture. The general ones are the easiest to isolate but again, because they are so commonplace, we are usually unaware of them.

Consider, for example, two aspects of posture, that crop up in the half-time scenario. Posture can provide an enormous amount of information. We can instantly recognize dominant or submissive stances in other people and we frequently employ them ourselves. When we wish to make an apology or plead for forgiveness we humble ourselves. Like chimpanzees we may literally 'bow and scrape' and we use our bodies to back up the verbal messages we give. So powerful is this non-verbal aspect that it can actually override a conflicting verbal meaning. We can often tell when people are hostile towards us even though they might say otherwise, because their bodies give them away. It is hard to maintain hypocrisy indefinitely. In fights the reading of perhaps unintentionally communicated body signals is an unconscious art which is undoubtedly handed down to us, in part, through evolution. It is not something we have to learn from scratch.

One of the most clear-cut symbols of hostility is the stare. At the beginning of the half-time scenario rival fans 'eye each other up' from a distance. As the distance between them decreases, they look sideways at each other. A stare at close quarters constitutes an unequivocal challenge to which one must respond or, in the context of aggro, lose face. Consequently, one only uses such a symbol sparingly and at times when the odds have been carefully assessed. Analogies with animal behaviour will be dealt with later but we might note at this stage how basic the stare is as a symbol of hostility in other primate species. Staring at chimps, for example, can often result in a full-flight charge. If you sharply look away as it hurtles forward, it will stop in its tracks. As the symbol of hostility is switched off the attack behaviour cuts out and the chimp reverts to grooming or to whatever he was doing at the time.

Football fans are cautious with their stares. As the latter part of our scenario illustrates, the victim avoids eye-contact with his assailant. But note, too, that the antagonist is actively searching for the victim's symbol of challenge. He wants him to stare because without this signal he cannot complete the sequence of action. He therefore seizes the slightest hint of eye-contact – even the inadvertent glance – in order to legitimate his actions and to oblige his victim to respond. Having detected such a signal, however unreasonably, the antagonist must succeed in manipulating the situation to his own ends. His victim must acknowledge that he himself has picked up the symbolic gauntlet by returning a hostile message. He cannot retort 'no, I wasn't staring' because that would lead either to the reply 'you calling me a liar?' or 'who do you think you're arguing with?' The victim's position is as constrained as if he were in check on the chess board.

The acceptance of the challenge is easily communicated. By turning and 'squaring up' his intention is understood. As a side-effect, his reputation is enhanced and it is here that we begin to see how such signals can have secondary meanings or exist at a different level. At the primary level the 'come-on-then' posture simply communicates the readiness for fighting. But, because of the set of values to which he and his fellows subscribe, his actions symbolize a certain laudable aspect of his character. Within his culture 'having a go' or demonstrating a limited degree of fearlessness confirms his status as 'a bit of a lad'. He's one of the boys – someone who will stick up for himself. After all, he could have fled or called for help. Without a set of values which hold in esteem acts of bravery, his stance might actually have resulted in censure. In other microcultures he might, for example, have been expected to turn his other cheek, or to sacrifice himself in the name of some higher ideal.

The bare patterns of behaviour, the postures, the facial expressions and the combinations of movements take on specific meanings because the encounter takes place in a particular social context. The communication of hostility and challenge takes on a new significance and entering into conflict can have pay-offs far beyond those of simply putting down a person who has been identified as a rival. The two levels of symbolic action work together. The socially realized symbols, as opposed to those which are biologically rooted, form part of a framework in which everyday events can be understood and in which personal character can be enhanced.

This might sound rather complicated, but in fact the point here is both fundamental and quite simple. We have to examine aggro at two levels. Firstly, at the level of elements of behaviour – what actions are involved; what are bovver boys actually doing? Secondly, we have to ask what these bits of behaviour mean. What secondary values do certain sequences of activity take on, and how do these values fit into the general scheme of things within a particular miniature social world?

Turning back again to the half-time scenario, the final sequence of behaviour looks unremarkable. The two fans just stand there. They throw no punches, they don't kick each other – they don't make any physical contact at all. And yet, the crowd around them would call this whole episode a 'fight'. They wouldn't talk about the lads who just looked at each other. The description of the event moves from the primary level of body signals to the secondary level where action is interpreted, made sense of and given value. The account is based on references to 'showing people what you're made of', 'having a go', 'demonstrating courage' and so on. Fighting becomes something other than a mere exchange of physical contacts.

From even the most cursory look at seemingly inconsequential encounters, an elementary principle emerges – a principle which is not based on some abstract, academic jargon but one which dictates how we must set about the task of unravelling the essential nature of conflict, hostility, and violence in its various guises.

An understanding of aggro must come through the examination of processes which are essentially human. We cannot afford to ignore parallels between what groups of men do and what happens in other species. In fact, a section of this book is devoted to comparisons between aggro in man and the resolution of conflict in animals. But such comparisons must come after the characteristically human social mechanisms have been teased out and examined. Having revealed the social order we might subsequently proceed to ask if such order is founded on regularities which are in our nature. But to rush straight into questions of this sort, without having filled in the elements of aggro at the social level, is a strategy which inevitably leads to quite false assumptions about the nature of human behaviour.

Man shares with other animals a certain genetic endowment. What he does and what he is able to do are both shaped and limited by the biological equipment he inherits. But we don't know very much about the way in which genetic mechanisms work and we know even less about their control over our behaviour. Despite the fact that thousands of books and learned papers have been written on the subject, we can conclude only one thing: our genetic endowment has only a very diffuse influence on the kinds of people we become and the ways in which we behave. One ethologist talks of the 'genetic suggestion' and this would seem to be a very sound idea to follow. Genetic factors lay down some broad directions but people, unlike other animals, are, by nature, capable of producing quite new directions. These directions appear at the secondary level and owe their power to the fact that we are social animals. We, for instance, can make use of an evolutionary novelty – language.

Words are things which set human aggro on a totally different level from the patterns of orderly conflict resolution to be found in other animals. The words do not operate in isolation from the primary messages we communicate with our faces and with our bodies. Verbal language may even be less effective as a communication channel in certain circumstances. But language and secondary symbols allow us to make aggro meaningful.

People do not act in a particular manner solely because of instinct or because they have a set of built-in reactions to certain objects or events around them. They do things in the light of the interpretations they make concerning both the actions of others and the situations in which these take place. In other words, people are deciding what things mean before they decide what to do, rather than blithely responding on the basis of a wired-in programme.

Again this might sound very complicated (or perhaps very obvious). We do, however, develop a basic social mechanism which makes life easier for ourselves. Instead of having to work everything out from first principles, whenever we need to decide what to do we are able to refer to a set of commonly held social rules. The particular set of rules we follow will depend upon the social group of which we are a member. For the most part we will be unaware that these rules exist at all. But the realization will come when the rules are broken. In our half-time example we can begin to see that what is going on there is not only broadly constrained by basic aspects of human nature, but that the actions of individuals are directed by a set of easily identifiable social conventions. Rules and conventions are more than mere reflections of regularities in behaviour – they have power. In everyday social life, even today, we observe many essential aspects of etiquette. When someone says 'good morning' we return the greeting. It's expected of us – we ought to do it. In the same way aggro has its own associated social etiquettes. Contrary to popular mythology, football fans don't kick to oblivion the first rival that crosses their path. Instead, they are constrained by protocols which are every bit as elaborate as those of French duelling. They are in evidence at the level of individual and small group conflict, but become even more apparent when we examine large groups and their conflicts. Our friends the football hooligans provide us with a third scenario which illustrates this point. This example is necessarily longer than the others because more is going on. But we can again zoom in on pieces of the action in order to reveal both levels of symbolic action. In longer scale conflicts we once more see aspects of order which, for reasons which will become apparent, seem rooted in human nature, and those which are maintained by social rules that are highly specific to the football-terrace culture.

The scene here is the 'warm-up' period at a football game. It is 2.15 on a Saturday afternoon and the home fans are already beginning to fill their 'End' even though there are another forty-five minutes before the match starts. 'Ends' are special. They are the sacred pieces of terracing which young loyal supporters have colonized for their exclusive use. Visiting supporters set foot on such hallowed ground at great peril to themselves. In the last ten years or so, Ends have become even more distinctive because the police and club officials have erected large steel fences around them in order to isolate the inhabiting rowdies from the rest of civilization. In the process, they have reinforced their special identities to a degree that the fans themselves could never have done. When we get excited about violence at football matches it is to the occupants of Ends that we refer. Other areas of the football ground contain mere spectators.

The warm-up period provides an opportunity for fans to rehearse their entire repertoire of symbolic patterns of behaviour. If we look closely at the chants and styles of hand-clapping something very interesting emerges. Firstly, as soon as the crowd on the terrace reaches what we might call a 'critical density' it suddenly takes on a very marked unity. The number of people required to achieve this critical density varies a lot but a minimum of about 100 fans is required. At the big grounds the critical level might be well over a thousand and little will happen on the terraces until it is reached. Below the critical level there are isolated and sporadic bursts of chanting and singing, but there is no cohesion in it. Songs die away in the middle and chants somehow fail to have any real impact. But as unity is achieved, activities such as staccato hand-clapping take on a precision which is probably higher than that achieved by well-drilled military bands. One way of measuring this precision is through the use of high-speed film techniques. Anyone with a reasonably good super 8 camera with variable speed settings can do this himself quite easily.

The cine-camera which is focused on the terracing normally runs at between eighteen and twenty-four frames per second. A standard projector runs the film back at the same speed. This means that if we compare a single frame of film with the next one in sequence, the time between the two events we view will be about 1/18th of a second. When football fans are engaged in the clapping rhythms, which are usually integrated with specific chants, they hold their arms above their heads, so that even when the terrace is packed they are in full view of our camera. We can see the extent to which fans are in 'synch' with each other. At normal speed, the hands all move together and apart at exactly the same time. In one frame they will be all closing together, and in the next they will have met at the clap point. Now we look at a film which has been taken at sixty-four frames per second. If this film is projected at normal speed the action appears to be slowed down. In fact it would take over three seconds to view what, in reality, occurred in one second. More importantly, if we look at single frames they will now only be 1/64th of a second apart. Again we see quite clearly that the precision is still there. Of the group who are in view, virtually all have their hands in identical positions at a particular time. The 'degree of error' is only a few inches at the most. How this remarkable precision is achieved, within what most people would see as disordered rabble, is a mystery which we will leave for a while. For the moment we need only be concerned with the fact that symbolic conflict is conducted through a channel of communication which is orderly to an almost absurd extent.

On top of all this synchrony comes a language which has a number of outstanding features. One of these is the intention to instill both fear and a sense of inferiority. Chants come and go and are subject to sudden changes in fashion. But ones like ' YOU'RE GOING TO GET YOUR FUCKING HEAD KICKED IN' remain pretty constant. All of this seems very straightforward. But there are some much more subtle aspects to be explored. Because most of the repertoire is used up during the half-hour or so before the game, we have the opportunity to examine, in a fairly comprehensive manner, the actual content of all the chants. One has to listen carefully because their staccato nature often makes the words less intelligible. If you are a rival fan at these times, however, the message will be clear. The following are a few samples:

1 'In their Millwall slums
   They look in the dustbin for something to eat.
   They find a dead cat and they think it's a treat.
   In their Millwall slums.'

2 'There's gonna be a nasty accident!'

3 'Swindon boys, wank, wank, wank.
   Swindon boys, wank, wank, wank.'

4 'Oxford boys, we are here
   Shag your women and drink your beer.'

These are just some of the verbal messages communicated as songs and chants and directed at fans from the host team. There's nothing very remarkable about them you might suppose. And yet, the distinctive pattern of insult exchanges can tell us a great deal about the aggro itself. In a subtle way, they reveal a very interesting and seemingly quite basic aspect of the whole conflict resolution ceremony.

The first example is about social class. The message of the song is that rival fans of the South London team Millwall, are slum-dwellers; they are of a lower caste. For sociologists who see football aggro as a manifestation of working-class revolt, as the expression of alienation by working-class kids from the increasingly bourgeois control of their soccer heritage, songs like this pose a serious problem. There is no solidarity with the *Lumpenproletariat* here. There is, however, another aspect of the song which is of even more interest. That is the reference to eating cats.

To suggest that rivals eat, with distasteful relish, the corpses of long-dead domestic pets is to issue a very special kind of imprecation. In our society there is a very strong taboo about treating cats as food. This arises because the cat has a rather anomalous status in the way we divide animals into edible and non-edible categories. A rabbit is anatomically not at all dissimilar to the cat. We eat the rabbit and not the cat. The cat is not a free animal. It is a domestic pet like the dog or the budgerigar or the goldfish. The closeness of these animals to human social life gives them a special status. It makes them, in one respect at least, like people. And being like people they cannot be eaten even though they are perfectly edible. In fact, in other cultures where they are not surrounded with an aura of close domesticity they are regularly converted into nourishing and tasty meals.

To suggest that rival fans are cat-eaters is, therefore, to accuse them of breaking a strong and well-defined taboo. And this, in itself, portrays them as very special kinds of men. They become men one can justifiably attack and put down. The taboo against cat-eating, on the other hand is by no means the most dominant in Western society. It is certainly not as strong as that which proscribes incest in virtually all human cultures. Calling somebody a 'mother-fucker', on this scale, would appear far more drastic. And that's perhaps one of the indications that in the USA, where the term is most frequently used, the violence associated with male conflicts is often of a very different pattern from that which manifests itself on the soccer terraces in Britain. Taboos, and scurrilous allegations about rivals breaching them, crop up. But it is never the ultimate taboo. It is one that arises out of curious social anomalies rather than out of something which is essentially a prerequisite for the proper survival of an entire species.

The second example is a chant that really tells us a great deal about the nature of the conflict resolution at football grounds. 'There is going to be a nasty accident.' There can surely be no more powerful indicator of the existence of rules and order than a statement like this. It acknowledges that routine events are not accidental. They are not random but are directed by a social order which gives aggro structure and safety. It warns, jokingly, that the opposition had better watch out because one might not continue to observe the niceties and etiquette of normal fighting. The implications are, of course, fairly horrific. But in practice the implied threat is rarely followed up by the savage anarchy we might, at first, predict. The importance of the chant lies not so much in its implied prediction but in its acknowledgment of the facts that order exists and one is fully aware of the mutually agreed ways of doing things.

The chant itself is often sparked off by actions on the part of the opposition which are thought to be themselves breaches of the rules. An interesting piece of youth culture argot is used to describe such breaches – the behaviour is referred to as 'out-of-order'. Again, actions can only be out-of-order if there is a recognized order there in the first place. If all was aimless and purely senseless violence, such concepts could not possibly arise or achieve any currency.

The third and fourth examples should be taken together since there is a very obvious contrast here. The contrast has to do with a very important quality – masculinity. In example 3, Swindon boys are portrayed as wankers: little boys who masturbate because they are not manly enough to do anything else. One of the most powerful insult gestures current among aggro boys is that which is made by flicking the wrist with fingers curled as if they were holding something about one inch in diameter. In example 4, however, one's own group takes your women and drinks beer and you can't get much more manly than that. A contest for extreme masculinity is one which gives rise to chants more often than any other single issue. On the football terraces the number of verbal messages denigrating the sexual powers or maleness of the opposition is much greater than that of those which are to do with spurring one's team to victory.

The masturbation theme is particularly common, but it is far from being the only one which is aimed at achieving male superiority. Allegations of homosexuality are also fairly predictable and they are aimed not just at rival fans but also against the players of the opposing team.

Taunts of homosexuality are by no means limited to the social world of the football terraces. They are a very integral part of verbal abuse in contemporary youth culture generally, at least in Britain. One has only to look at the number of insult terms current in everyday language which directly imply homosexuality: 'poofter', 'queer', 'fairy', 'nancy', and so on. Again the aim of such terms is to belittle a rival's masculine status with a suggestion that he is incapable of a normal heterosexual way of life, and they play a very central role in all forms of aggro.

I am not, for one moment, suggesting that we should endorse such a pattern of activity or necessarily share the view that homosexuals are people to be decried and made targets for abuse. That is not the purpose of this kind of analysis at all. What I am trying to do, in effect, is to show up the basic processes on which orderly aggro is founded. And masculinity, with all that it entails in present-day youth culture, and whether we like it or not, is certainly a key factor. Within the context of ceremonial battles in and around soccer grounds manliness becomes larger than life.

Those who are seen as anything less than manly can sometimes become the objects of further ridicule and, very occasionally, violence. It is important to realize, though, that this pattern of ritual insult exchange often serves instead of physical violence. Putting down a rival can be achieved through the chants and the songs and thus the necessity for inflicting physical hurt falls away. One often hears such phrases as 'Leave him alone, he's just a wanker'. In other words, one has been so successful in attaching the ultimate humiliation to him that further action is not required. An even more effective barrier to violence is created when a rival is given the status of a female.

Aggro, as we have already seen, is an all-male affair. We will leave aside at present the thorny question of why women and girls in our society don't engage in this kind of activity. For the moment we will just take it for granted that they don't. Within the context of aggro, therefore, females are irrelevant – they form no part of the ceremony and, more importantly, they are not legitimate objects of attack. There is no conflict here except with other males. If then, in the process of ritual insult exchange, a rival can be effectively deprived of his male gender classification, he no longer poses a threat at all. Psychological castration renders him harmless.

The insult 'You silly girl' applied to other males has widespread currency in all walks of life. Feminists, of course, get very upset that allusions to being a woman should be insulting at all. From their point of view they are right to be indignant. But such allusions *are* insulting. It's one of the ultimate put-downs that a man can receive in our kind of male-dominated culture. It should come as no surprise, therefore, that soccer fans borrow from the dominant ideology this very basic method of humiliating fans of the opposing team. And again, the words do the work which might otherwise be done with knuckles and boots. 'Silly girls' are not worth bothering about, and they are certainly not legitimate targets for violence. The recipients of such epithets may, on the other hand, feel obliged to resist this image and to demonstrate that they are, contrary to the insult terms applied to them, true men. The ultimate feminizing term is one that always requires some reaction unless one is miserably to lose face altogether. That is the simple word 'cunt'.

The fact that cunt, a vulgarized description of the female pudendum, has come to be one of the fiercest terms of abuse in the whole verbal insult repertoire reinforces the point I have been making concerning masculinity as the primary issue of aggro. To be called a 'prick' is much less powerful. Indeed 'cock' is actually a term of endearment. But to be reduced to a female sex organ is the ultimate disaster. If your rival can get away with such a feat then you become as subdued as if you had been savagely beaten into the ground. Your status becomes zero and your claims to membership of the masculine culture are rendered unacceptable.

Stereotyped verbal insults form a kind of continuum. They range from rather mild references to generally proscribed personal habits, up to ones of absolute demasculinization. The weaker ones are often so lacking in vitriolic power that they can easily be used, in a light-hearted context, as tokens of friendship and camaraderie. There is, however, a distinct point on the continuum where the insult terms become single purpose and that point often occurs when the references of the terms are concerned with one's sexual identity. The fact that conflict resolution, of the type that occurs at football grounds, is centred around this distinctive style of insulting behaviour, tells us that aggro is quite different from other patterns of violence and hostile expression. Whilst football fans are engaged in an endless struggle to demasculinize each other, those involved in other kinds of violence – violence where maiming and killing are all too regular events – are often caught up in a quite different business – that of dehumanizing their fellow men. In all of the incessant abuse which is hurled across the football terraces every Saturday there are virtually no instances at all of calling into question a rival's claim to be a member of the human species. All other qualities may be called into question but not his status as a person.

The contrast between dehumanization and demasculinization, and the resulting differences in the manner in which people fight each other, is something which separates aggro from other forms of violence. This topic is discussed in more detail in Chapter 6.

It is interesting to note at the moment, though, that there is one rather special kind of dehumanizing activity which surrounds football aggro. It is to be found, perhaps unexpectedly, in the comments of those who are outraged about it all. Newspapers, the champions of this indignant section of society, reveal something which verges on the alarming in their statements about soccer fans. 'Chelsea fans are animals' runs a typical headline. The message is clear. Football hooligans are not be considered members of the same species as other clean-living folk. They are to be demoted to an inferior status: that of lower animals. Such reactions would seem to have very serious implications indeed, not least for the maintenance of aggro in our society as a positive social force.

The state of affairs has probably reached its ultimate peak in the most recent announcements of the press who suggest that merely expelling fans from *Homo sapiens* is not good enough. 'Soccer fans *worse* than animals' says one of the more recent headlines. Perhaps all those nice ladies with their poodles and their pekes were becoming upset by the suggestion that their expensively nurtured pets were in any way like those demons who regularly rampage through less fortunate neighbourhoods.

Leaving aside the insidious overtones of this whole media censure

29

though, we might take seriously for the moment this parallel between fans and animals. In doing so we might well consider whether aggro, the pattern of social hostility contained within a stylized framework, has any parallels in the animal kingdom. Unhappy magistrates, in denouncing those who appear before them as animalistic, might be showing great ignorance of what animals actually do and, in particular, how they fight one another. To call someone who regularly gets into the middle of aggro an animal might, ironically, be to make a highly pertinent and certainly not unfavourable analogy. Aggro on the terraces is very typical of the ceremonial fights and bundles we can find in many other areas of our society and, indeed, throughout much of the rest of the world. It may also be that the ways in which other animals solve conflicts and hostilities within their own species have more than a passing resemblance to the events we have studied so far.

2

Animal Rituals

Our introduction to aggro has been through a brief look at what goes on at football matches in Britain. For many people in this country, aggro and football hooliganism are synonymous. But if aggro was simply a feature peculiar to football fans – to particular groups of young people – there would be little point in pursuing this investigation much further. Sociologists would undoubtedly continue to write Ph.D. theses on this extraordinary feature of working-class existence and aggro would become a museum piece. Social historians in a few hundred years' time might reflect on the social curios of the late twentieth century, singling out the Teddy Boys – Mods and Rockers – Skinheads – football hooligans sequence as indicative of society's early attempts to live in an age where a world war had heralded an era of potential nuclear annihilation. This, however, is fantasy. As we will see, aggro has had a role to play in everyday life for as long as history has been recorded. Today it exists, as it has always existed, to provide a safe solution to the inevitable conflicts in which men find themselves.

Observers of animal behaviour have been familiar with this kind of thing for many years. In fact, they get very upset when they hear magistrates condemn football hooligans as behaving like animals. They know that the implied savage and senseless acts of violence are rarely characteristic of the animal species they study. If you talk to them about football aggro, in the sense that it is being taken here, they will immediately recognize what it is. Once you have convinced them that fans are not the raging band of maniacs they might, at first, appear they will identify their actions as being very much like the patterns of ritualized aggression which are found in virtually all other species of animal.

Aggression and ritualization are technical terms and are used by students of both animal and human behaviour in a quite specific way. The trouble here, though, is that scanning through the textbooks on human behaviour will reveal a large number of different definitions of aggression – many of which are quite incompatible with each other. Psychologists, in particular, are prone to inventing new classifications of aggression almost daily. The product of all this is a great deal of confusion. The problem of getting to grips with the concept in a proper manner seems to totally defeat some writers on the subject. Roger Johnson, for example, who wrote a very readable book called *Aggression in Man and Animals*, was happy to state that there was no single kind of behaviour which could be called aggressive nor, indeed, any single process which could be called aggression. To say that and then write a whole text on the subject is quite an achievement. Ashley Montagu, in his diatribe against notions of genes and instincts, ironically called *The Nature of Human Aggression*, is equally evasive. He provides a list of thirteen types of aggression, ranging from 'predatory aggression' through 'parental discipline' to 'irritable aggression'. But he fails to tell us what aggression is. He tells us that whatever it is, it is not genetically determined. But that isn't really good enough. When he comes, very briefly, to talk about ritualization he gets himself even more tied up in muddled statements such as: '. . . the purpose of . . . ritualized aggression is not aggression, but the achievement of the animal's object without physically harmful aggression.' Quite clearly, this is an unsatisfactory start to understanding the very real problems of everyday aggression between men in contemporary society. We have to do better than this, particularly if we are to leave open the possibility of learning something about ourselves from studies of animal behaviour. A more reasonable starting point for understanding aggression might come not from textbooks but from the use of the term in informal, lay talk.

We all have a vague idea of what aggression means and we use the term in a non-technical way very frequently. And what is most interesting about such usage is that it tends not to be limited to things like fighting and violence. We talk of the aggressive salesman – the dynamic, go-ahead young man determined to progress quickly up the ladder of promotion. We also refer to athletes who run aggressive races and to sportsmen who display competitive aggression in a struggle to score goals and win matches. In these cases we also imply that the aggression is worthy of some admiration. In contrast, we can use the word aggression in a very pejorative sense. 'Unbridled aggression', a stock phrase of some journalists, is often used as a damning comment on the activities of hooligans, tearaways and delinquent gangs. Here the connection between aggression and violence is seen as being immediate and therefore unwelcome. The fact that it is seen as being uncontrolled makes it the target of censure.

This might all sound a bit too woolly to be of real value but the fact that we can use the idea of aggression independently without necessarily talking of violence in the sense of inflicting physical hurt is very important. We can be aggressive without causing pain and, equally, we can cause a great deal of suffering without actually being aggressive. Consider the man who flies in a large aeroplane over a heavily populated city and releases a lethal cargo of high explosives. The results of his actions are death and incalculable misery. But when he presses the button he can be calm, unemotional and detached. He can't even see the city he will destroy and his action is as devoid of aggression as posting a letter in a pillar box.

Aggression, then, is independent of any specific event. Violence may be a consequence of aggression but it is by no means an automatic consequence. Nor is aggression an inevitable precondition for an act of violence. Rather aggression might be viewed as the intentional process of subduing or achieving dominance over a rival. The athlete does this by running faster, and the footballer by scoring more goals or making an effective tackle. The young thug might do it by smashing a bottle over his opponent's head. The outcomes are the same but the means are very different. It is the means for resolving aggression, however, which are the major concern here. And one of the means which is strikingly prevalent within the world of animals is that of ritual display which is substituted for lethal onslaught.

Virtually all species of animal are aggressive. And they show aggression for reasons which appear to be very sound. Firstly, aggression allows for the establishment and maintenance of relatively stable patterns of dominance and submission. Secondly, the process is involved in territorial defence, resulting in optimum dispersal of animals in relation to the resources available in their environment. Some species have more rigidly structured dominance hierarchies than others and there is also great variation in the extent to which animals are territorial. But aggression is common to all and it is one of the things which keeps them in the survival game. At the same time, however, it presents a problem because of its destructive potential. Rivals need to be subdued and trespassers repelled. But if such activities regularly resulted in death and serious wounding a species would soon find itself on the verge of extinction. Not only would the population decline as a result of the increased fatality rate but the basic dominance networks would rapidly fall apart. You can't very well dominate another male if you have killed him. And if, in the process, you have also been seriously wounded then an easy target is presented for other ambitious rivals in the group. The solution here is ritualization. By turning the whole conflict business into an aggressive ritual, fights become stylized games and displays – things which bear an uncanny resemblance to the events we saw going on at the football ground tea-stall.

Put simply, ritualization, in this context, refers to the process whereby patterns of attacking behaviour become modified through the process of evolution so that they are what one eminent ethologist has referred to as 'ritual tournaments'. Most species have patterns of attack behaviour which are generally thought to be, at least in part, innate and don't have to be learned. What ritualization does is to maintain these responses but cut them short or modify them so that they become relatively harmless. By way of an introduction to ritual fighting among animals, we might do well to start with the humble lizard and with the observations provided by Konrad Lorenz.

The particular lizards in question are of the species *Lacerta agilis*. Two males are faced with the problem of solving a conflict between them. The combat begins when each lizard adopts a broadside position with respect to the other. Their narrow bodies are parallel but they face in opposite directions. This narrowness of their bodies becomes exaggerated through contraction of the rib cage. In effect, this means that as they stand head to tail the outlines of their bodies are very marked. Such lizards also have a distinctive colouring on the flanks and belly. Through the active narrowing and heightening movements, yellow and green bands are pulled up into a vertical position on the sides of their bodies and present a display which is unmistakably one of threat. This display might last for some time – both lizards showing their colours but remaining motionless. Eventually each lizard turns its head to the other offering it as a target. This may sound a little injudicious but lizards have a very tough covering and are well protected in this area. The reptile which takes the first bite, observe the ethologists, is usually the weaker or the smaller of the two. In many cases, it seems that the battle has been lost or won by this stage, and the bite is no more than a token gesture for the vanquished lizard before he capitulates and takes up a surrendering posture. Where the two are more evenly matched, on the other hand, the fight might last longer: each in strict order bites the head of the other. Lorenz notes that neither he nor other observers of the *Lacerta agilis* ever witnessed a conflict in which these lizards bit any other area of their opponents' bodies or made an attack out of turn. He also points out that this kind of ritual is not limited to the one species.

The same is true in *Lacerta strigata major*, in which, most surprisingly, the males grab at each other at the proffered knee and, thus linked in a circular arrangement, dance round each other in a wrestling match strongly reminiscent of a certain Swiss national sport, the 'Hosenwrangeln'. ('Ritual Fighting')

The consequence of these lizard tournaments is that neither combatant gets killed. The whole encounter may end with a single token bite or may continue until one protagonist becomes tired and declares that he has had enough. Where the conflict involves possession of a particular territory the loser will slide off leaving his victor to his own kingdom. The problem is solved. Both lizards are undamaged. And, as a consequence, one reptile is forced to colonize an extra piece of the environment. We would be hard pressed to design a system that worked as effectively as this, given that aggression was inherent in the male of the species.

It may seem a big jump from lizards to people, and indeed it is. Nobody, unless he is very foolhardy, is going to suggest that the factors which influence and determine the behaviour of the lowly lizard are at all the same as those which form the basis of our own actions. On the other hand, to ignore, for whatever reason, the striking parallels between ritualized animal fighting and the stylized structure of contemporary aggro in human societies would seem unnecessarily chauvinistic. We might say that, by and large, animals have nature and man has culture. But cultures don't simply materialize out of fresh air. They must be founded upon something that is in our nature – in our physical make-up. However much we try to get round the unpalatable fact, we are forced to admit that whatever else we might be, we have trodden the path through evolution upon which the lizard still scuttles. Being 'persons' means we have gone beyond many of the restrictions which still hold captive the lower animals. But in going beyond, we still take with us something of our primal heritage. We adapt it, we modify it, we control it, and eventually our lives and our societies take on new qualities. The qualities, though, still have their foundations – the building blocks which support the entire edifice.

All this is by way of preempting the now traditional reaction which greets anybody so foolish as to suggest that people share with other animals some basic aspects of their nature. Equally it is an early warning to those who smugly welcome in such comparisons the thesis that man's behaviour can be understood in precisely the same limited range of concepts which are thought adequate for making sense of, say, the laboratory rat. Neither thesis, nor the by no means logically related political doctrines which habitually accompany them, are to be allowed much room here. What is required, but rarely found, is an attempt to see how comparisons between the actions of people and the behaviour of animals can be incorporated in a framework which has implications for the understanding of contemporary violence in our societies. If this attempt fails it will not be for lack of putting aside one's own social and political leanings.

Lorenz's example suggests a neatly tailored mechanism for coping with male aggression in a given species. The mechanism, however, is only of adaptive value if aggression is a fixed and necessary feature of that species. A more straightforward way of getting around the problem would be to breed out aggression and evolve species in which members live in passive cooperation with each other. As we will discover, there are some very good reasons why this solution is never achieved in reality in any species that has yet been discovered.

It must be said that not all animals have evolved such neat solutions to the problems of aggression. Even other kinds of lizard, such as *Lacerta mellisselensis*, differ from their ceremonial cousins in that they regularly kill each other in fights. But these, most students of animal behaviour would agree, are exceptions to the normal pattern of things. The vast majority of species, to a greater or lesser extent, have evolved distinctive ritual answers to the question of survival. But how is this ritualization achieved and what characterizes its development? To answer these questions we need to look closely at some of the more recent conclusions concerning the process of evolution and how ritualization of behaviour fits in to the universal order of nature itself.

Any discussion of evolution must, at least, acknowledge the impetus provided by Charles Darwin – a name synonymous with the politicized rhetoric of 'survival of the fittest'. Darwin has had a bad press during the last thirty years, mainly due to the pronouncements of the so-called neo-Darwinists. In the same way as the writings of Marx and Engels have been 'up-dated' by a whole kaleidoscope of left-wing successors, so the works of Darwin have been taken as a justification for all kinds of extreme right-wing and totalitarian philosophies. Today the neo-Marxists and neo-Darwinists stand at opposite ends of the political spectrum. But Marx, in fact, was a great admirer of Darwin's approach to the study of man. Although he disagreed with some of the details of his research strategies, he was sufficiently in accord with his view to consider dedicating *Das Kapital* to Darwin. Such is the way of political bigots, however, that the path to rational understanding is abandoned in favour of simplistic slogans.

One of Darwin's singular, but often ignored, contributions to the explanation of animal behaviour was his insistence that animals, at least those relatively high up on the evolutionary ladder, have emotions. Put simply, animals can become aggressive or sexy or frightened and their behaviour can only be understood as being consequent upon such emotions. A simple thought, perhaps, but one which, if accepted, radically alters the way in which we treat the whole subject of animal ethology.

A study of evolution becomes something rather more than the study of physical and biological changes, reflected in anatomical organizations. It becomes also the investigation of the way in which subjective experiences can be organized into new distinct forms. A physical world fuels the chemical changes which are responsible for the developing physical structure of all animal species. But experience of the physical world also alters the way in which animals behave and respond to particular problematic situations. This point is developed at some length by Sir Julian Huxley. Again it might seem a rather obvious idea, but, sadly, scientists are not always amenable to common sense. At times they prefer to pursue lines of investigation which, although scientifically very rigorous, seem to have little meeting point with everyday experience. Some of them, on the other hand, lean in the opposite direction and attribute all sorts of essentially human characteristics to even the simplest of animals. This anthropomorphic approach can lead to even greater problems unless kept in check. Attributing basic emotion to animals is one thing, but doing much more can be hazardous. This will become clear when we deal with the manner in which comparisons between animals and people can legitimately be made. Since animals, unlike people, do not have language, nor the conceptual powers that linguistic ability brings, there has to be a point at which comparative studies become meaningless. We have to be very careful that this limit is not passed in our quest for a more adequate understanding of violence.

The idea that evolution proceeds through the joint processes of organic adaptation and organization of subjective experience, brings us nearer to an approach which makes sense when applied to people. For us, culture plays a dominant role by providing a framework in which our experiences can be interpreted and realized. To speak of animals having culture in this sense would not be appropriate. In ritualization, however, we see the beginnings of a modification of the total restrictions of pre-programmed behaviour.

Most animals have instinctive reactions, based on fear, to certain potentially dangerous situations. At the simplest level of ritualization it is these patterns which become modified. But not only do they become less injurious to other members of the species, they come to serve as distinct signals in their own right. As such they provide a basis for a primary symbolic system. In the lizard tournament, the yellow stripes, made more visible through the expression of aggression and hostility, stand as threat displays. It is the development of such symbols, effective only within a given species, which provides the basic materials for subsequent evolutionary sophistication and ultimately for the creation of symbolic systems in man. Without such a foundation, the social order and tacit rules of conflict resolution, which we witness on the soccer terraces and elsewhere, would be impossible to construct. Unless threat and displays have somehow come to stand in place of mortal combat, fights could hardly have evolved into the ceremonial and gentlemanly institutions which have occupied a place in our history for as long as we care to remember.

The emergence of ritualized threat signals has taken a variety of forms and in many species particular parts of the body seem specially engineered to transmit such signals. In male sticklebacks, for example, the belly area changes to a vivid red colour in the mating season. It seems that at this time of the year such fish need to clearly warn off rival males who threaten their breeding territories. The red belly does just this and also serves to arouse aggression among nearby male members of the same species. It warns and threatens just as effectively as the clenched human fist. In the case of the stickleback the reaction to the red belly is not something which is learned. Young sticklebacks which have been reared in isolation from each other and from their elders still show the same reaction to the signal, even though they have had no opportunity to learn its significance. The red belly constitutes what ethologists call an 'innate releaser' – it automatically evokes fixed responses. In such cases, the actual signals provided need not even be real. Experiments have shown that very crude models can be used to elicit the same behaviour. The models work even without major features such as fins attached to them so long as the underside is appropriately coloured. These releasers are truly 'the red rag to the bull'. Whilst red rags don't, in fact, do much for bulls because they are colour-blind, red bellies are the things that immediately put sticklebacks into physiological overdrive.

Similar signals are to be found in conflicts between male *Betta splendens*, more familiarly known as the Siamese fighting fish. But here the mere presence of another male conspecific is enough to send it into an apparently senseless rage. It will even attack its own image in a mirror. The pattern of fighting here is again very stylized and although minor injuries are quite common, actual deaths from these fights are very rare. Once more highly distinctive threat displays come to serve in the place of total savagery.

The gill-covers of the Siamese fighting fish are extended out from the body as soon as a rival male approaches. Fins and tail stiffen to their maximum dimensions and the resulting spectacle is made even more unmistakable by an intensification of the body colouring itself. The display is followed by rigorous tail-waggling by both combatants – the general aim seemingly that of trying to convince the rival he has less energy and is certainly much smaller. This in itself may be sufficient to drive off a male interloper. Where some actual fighting occurs, perhaps because the two fish are fairly evenly matched, they will ram each other or attempt to tear each other's fins until one is forced to retreat.

Such automatic reactions as these, which have become safely stereotyped through the process of ritualization, stand out as the most simple and straightforward answers to the problems of aggression. Certain signals switch on hostile behaviour, and when the conflict has been satisfactorily resolved, other signals switch it off. But what of animals that are a little higher up the evolutionary ladder – those a little nearer to man himself?

Inevitably, as we begin to examine ritualized fighting in species which have emerged rather later in the history of nature the picture becomes more complex. Some quite fundamental processes, however, can be isolated without too much trouble through straightforward observation of their everyday behaviour. One such process, which appears to be a very basic aspect of ritualized aggression in the higher animals, is the introduction of irrelevant behaviour into the conflict situation. Desmond Morris, in his now almost legendary book *The Naked Ape*, outlines with great clarity examples of these irrelevant activities.

There is another important source of special signals arising from a category of behaviour that has been named displacement activity. One of the side effects of intense inner conflicts is that an animal sometimes exhibits strange and seemingly irrelevant pieces of behaviour. It is as if the tensed-up creature, unable to perform either of the things it is desperate to do (i.e.

39

fight or run away) finds an outlet for its pent up energy in some other, totally unrelated activity

Examples of this kind of activity are to be found in such things as incomplete feeding behaviour. In the middle of a threat posture an animal will break off and momentarily scratch for food, returning to the business of challenging his rival as quickly as he left it. Similarly ethologists have observed brief nest-building activities or even momentary 'sleeping' in the middle of aggressive encounters. According to Desmond Morris, these seemingly bizarre activities are all part and parcel of the ritualization process and become an intrinsic part of the primary system of symbolic communication whose function is to defuse hostile encounters to the extent where they can be resolved without serious bloodshed. The whole elaborate ceremony, with its repertoire of threats, hostile signals, displacements and submission postures, is perhaps best exemplified in contests between rival chimps.

It must be said that the chimp is not a particularly aggressive species when compared with other animals. But the relative peace that chimps enjoy is kept very much in existence by a distinct dominance hierarchy among male members. The maintenance of this framework doesn't simply depend on the elementary and automatic fixed responses which are characteristic of many species of fish and reptiles. On the contrary, many of the signals and displays which make up the chimp ritual repertoire appear to be context-specific; they depend upon the particular situation in which rival males find themselves.

One of the best accounts of chimp tournaments is given by Jane Van Lawick-Goodall in her study of the Gombe Stream Reserve in Tanzania. The animals she observed were free-living and unconstrained and roaming around in perfectly natural habitats. Her detailed investigations allowed her to isolate the following major aspects of threat behaviour which were combined in an endless variety of ways in different situations, but were unmistakably the basic elements of the chimps' ritual system for coping with intraspecific aggression.

The stare was one of the most common elements, sometimes accompanied by head-jerking movements but on other occasions simply constituting a motionless glare. Hair erection, a frequent physiological reaction to fear and stress in many species, often accompanied the glaring. Arms were brought into play, waved high above the head as the chimps stood erect or even ran around on hind legs. The feet would sometimes be used to stamp the ground whilst hooting and screaming at the enemy in front. Occasionally, one chimp would break away from this kind of display and start to vigorously shake the smaller branches of a nearby tree or bush. From time to time, an angry chimp would engage in the most blatant and recognizable sign of hostility one can imagine. He would pick up rocks lying around on the ground and hurl them at his rival. These primitive weapons rarely caused serious injury but were very effective in forcing an opponent to retreat.

In describing this pattern of activity in words, a lot of the true impact of the energetic spectacle is lost. Even when watching it on film the whole reality and immediate relevance of this ceremonial pattern of behaviour somehow escapes you. It wasn't until I was fortunate enough to visit the chimp colony at Arnhem Zoo in Holland that I suddenly realized how much the aggro I was becoming very familiar with on Saturday afternoons had in common with these primate rituals.

At Arnhem, Jan van Hooff runs an open colony for a tribe of chimps who lead as normal an existence as is possible given that they are in captivity. They are not caged or fenced in. Instead they are marooned on an island and surrounded by a kind of moat. Isolated in this way they live very much as they might have done in the wild and it is here that one can observe, in close-up and in great detail over a long period of time, the management of everyday problems and basic factors such as aggression. It was here that it was possible to see at first hand, in my case for the first time, the precise way in which chimps skilfully head off the strutting advances of males eager to ensure that their dominant position in the social hierarchy is strongly reaffirmed and maintained.

Adopting a submissive posture is the clearest way in which an animal, and indeed a person for that matter, can signal that he has had enough and thus avoid serious injury. The chimp makes such signals in a variety of ways, one of the most common being a whimpering response which is accompanied with an open mouth and lip retraction which serves fully to expose the teeth. Literal 'bowing and scraping' is another very common way of indicating submission. The defeated chimp lowers his body and runs a hand along the ground in a posture of complete subservience and humility.

The introduction of sexual behaviour as a heading-off tactic adds a new twist to the whole conflict resolution business. Quite frequently the submissive male will engage in a classic 'presenting' display; offering himself for sexual mounting to his rival in exactly the same way that a female presents herself to her mate. In some

41

instances the dominant male will actually mount his vanquished inferior and engage in a few desultory pelvic thrusts. The introduction of a competing drive serves effectively to put an end to the whole affair. It becomes a sex game. In the process the hierarchical relationships are kept intact and neither animal is in the least way physically harmed. In fact, the whole display usually ends with the dominant male himself making some appeasement gestures. Having clearly beaten his rival he may then proceed to pat him on the head, hold his hand or even kiss him.

It is very easy to become anthropomorphic here and to ascribe essentially human characteristics to animals such a chimps – especially when their behaviour seems to resemble our own so closely. The pattern of threat, submission and appeasement seems particularly near to our own experiences of quarrels and struggles against our competitors. When we shake hands, pat each other on the back, wave or remonstrate we seem to be engaged in activities that our primate cousins would understand well. And watching chimps fighting each other in the colony in Arnhem one could, without a great stretch of the imagination, see them with scarves around their wrists charging energetically around the Ends at Tottenham or Chelsea.

One thing that chimps lack, however, is the power of language to aid their ceremonial patterns of aggression management. They don't have the rich repertoire of insults which in man can do the work of physical displays or even of violence itself. But in all other respects it is not unreasonable to assume that the primary elements of aggro owe much to the styles of behaviour that are so clearly displayed in chimpanzee communities. And if anyone doubts that primate aggro is based on anything other than the considerations of masculinity which are uppermost in the struggles between rival men, they should watch a male baboon as he waves his erect penis at rival interlopers as a clear and defiant warning.

To some, the baboon and his peculiar habits might seem a rather distasteful creature. To run around doing that kind of thing in our modern society would certainly win you very few friends and would undoubtedly get you arrested. In many other cultures, on the other hand, the erect penis has played a rather special role in the management of conflict. Papuan tribesmen, for example, use special sheaths over their genitals in battle. The function of these is not merely to serve as protection of a rather vital part of the body, but specifically to exaggerate the size of the penis itself. Those worn by some warriors are so long that they have to be supported by a kind of harness worn around the waist which maintains the erect position. Among other societies the symbolism of the erect penis is so strong that it has found representation in amulets or charms with protective significance. As a symbol of aggressive threat it appears in some of the pictures on the walls of Egyptian tombs and was, presumably, designed to warn away trespassers. On the island of Nias, wooden carvings of men, which are very crude except for the accurately carved phallus, stand outside houses to protect the occupants from potential foes. The Ancient Greeks, it seems, had exactly the same kind of guardians, but here carved in stone. The baboon might have a lot to answer for.

The fact that the erect penis crops up as a symbolic warning device in some human cultures, and also figures strongly in the way a baboon threatens his rival, may be totally coincidental. If this was all there was to it, if there were no other similarities between human and animal conflict resolution and management, there would be little point in pursuing the issue at all. But when the parallels keep building up, when the similarities become so immediately striking and precise even in small details, then we really are forced to take notice of them.

In looking at the antics of soccer fans I tried to pave the way for subsequent comparisons with other kinds of aggro. I suggested that there was one level of activity that could be equated with animal behaviour and I think that the cursory look at primate behaviour reinforces the point. In the often ignored ceremonies of small group confrontations in human life are to be seen many of the primary signals which are so typical of the way rival male chimps cope with their problems of dominance and submission. The stare, the distinctive postures, the cautious jumping backwards and forwards, the whimpering and the arm flailing – they seem so central to the course of action on both the soccer terraces and Jan van Hooff's chimp island. This kind of comparison is legitimate and it is fruitful. It suggests very strongly that these basic aspects of human behaviour are not 'pathological' as some behavioural scientists would have us believe. They are not the products of disturbed personality or social impoverishment in boys and young men any more than they are in the case of other male primates. They are, in fact, perfectly normal aspects of behaviour. No matter how much we dislike them, and no matter how much we try, in the name of civilization and cultural progress, to eradicate them, we are forced to acknowledge their inevitability and indeed their positive value. They are the cornerstones on which a way of coping with male aggression has been achieved by generation after generation of culture builders. If we fail to recognize this, and if we continue to be ignorant of what

43

underlies the whole business of aggro, we may be in for a nasty shock.

The animal studies can't tell us anything directly about the secondary level of aggression management. There is no one-to-one link here with, say, highly specialized patterns of verbal exchange and the rudimentary hooting of angry chimps. But the study of other animals can give us clues to some central aspects which appear on a secondary and social plane in human action. The theme of sex again seems an appropriate one to pursue.

In listening closely to chants and songs on the soccer terraces, sex cropped up frequently and in a very special way. Many of the terms used made explicit reference to non-heterosexual activity and seemed to have the function of turning the 'enemy' into 'non-men': of taking away their masculine status. At the extremes, we saw that certain forms of insult appeared to have the function of feminizing a rival. There is no directly comparable behaviour in other animal species, but there are many aspects of their behaviour which seem very consistent with this whole scheme of things. The submissive chimp becomes like a female in order to escape punishment. By taking away his own masculinity he removes the major source of conflict. The dominant chimp is no longer threatened.

Now vanquished soccer fans don't go around pointing their bottoms at other rival supporters. Nor do the victors engage in the pelvic thrusting movement of the dominant chimp. Language and gesture have taken over completely here, and the primary patterns of behaviour are discarded in favour of new, socially prescribed ways of doing things. Elsewhere in the world, however, the memory of primate presenting action lives on. The Japanese, for example, have special amulets which are used as tokens of deference and appeasement. And what form do these amulets take? They are rather crude carvings of a female rump stuck up in the air and serving as an unmistakable invitation.

From lizards to fish to chimps and finally man himself we can observe a process which, whilst increasing in complexity and variation, is quite central to the common problem of survival. In drawing out the parallels we could have considered the rattlesnakes who, though partial to American settlers, never bite each other. In addition, lengthy descriptions of ritual fighting among birds might have been considered or attention given to the detailed accounts of dogs and wolves ceremonially nipping each other and urinating as a token of submission. But this is not a book on animal ethology. The aim is to come closer to an understanding of human aggression. And that involves general, rather than specific, comparisons with how other animals behave. Football bovver boys or Punks or *blousons noirs* do what they do for reasons which are to be found within the complex but informal social institutions in which they act. The rituals in which they engage are arbitrary and the secondary symbols which characterize their aggressive displays and exchanges are often peculiar to specific arenas. But underlying them all is the same fundamental process.

Comparisons between human social life and the behaviour of our nearest primate cousins, even at a general level, are seductive. They form the basis of some of the best-selling books in recent years. But we can all too easily be carried away by them, by the idea that man is nothing more than a clever ape who has lost his hair. The suggestion that complex secondary aspects of man's social behaviour, in particular those which centre around the use of language and verbal communication, can be explained in the same limited range of concepts appropriate to the study of other species, is something which must be resisted very strongly. The object of the exercise here is not to reduce people to the level where their behaviour can be readily matched up with that of the chimp or even the Siamese fighting fish. Rather, it is to return to the basic point made earlier that human social frameworks and patterns of symbolic action do not emerge, as if by magic, out of a total void. They are the result of man's exceptional ability to build on nature rather than remaining enslaved by it. If we ever want to get to grips with and make sense of these complicated social structures, we have to understand the foundations upon which they are erected. To do this we also need to look at what are thought to be more 'primitive' forms of human culture. Not only are our roots in the world of nature, our social heritage is to be found in the world of tribes and communities unburdened by technological sophistication. Having noted the findings of ethology, our understanding of contemporary aggro now requires attention to be paid to the work of anthropologists.

3

Tribal Rituals

The Dani are a tribe of plains people in New Guinea. Some years ago they became famous through the work of anthropologist film makers Robert Gardner and Karl Heider. The film *Dead Birds*, made in 1963, provided the Western world with a vivid account of life in a warrior community – of life where battles were almost everyday features of social life. Writing about them some years later Robert Gardner had this to say:

> The Dani fight because they want to and because it is necessary. They do not enter into battle in order to put an end to fighting. They do not envisage the end of the fighting any more than the end of gardening or ghosts. Nor do they fight in order to annexe land or to dominate people. The Dani are warriors because they have wanted to be since boyhood, not because they are persuaded by political arguments or their own sentimental patriotic feelings. They are ready to fight whenever their leader decides to do so. (*Gardens of War*)

Dani culture is steeped in conflict between a dozen or so tribes which constitute the plains population. But, as Gardner reports, wars among the rival factions do not arise at regular intervals. They occur when influential warrior leaders decide that it is about time for a battle or a raid on a nearby village.

Such decisions are not taken on the basis of the same kind of logical reasons which are supposed (perhaps wrongly) to lie at the root of such matters in the so-called 'civilized' Western world. Instead a Dani leader pays heed to the potential holocaust which might ensue if ghosts are unavenged. All that happens in the New Guinea villages is as a result of the influence of the ghosts who are a totally accepted aspect of everyday folk culture. If things go wrong, if someone has an accident or the crops fail, then the ghosts are troubled and something needs to be done about it. Pure superstition, we might think in our civilized manner of dismissing all things irrational. Marvin Harris on the other hand, who wrote a book called *Cows, Pigs, Wars and Witches*, has shown that what often seems to be highly unreasonable behaviour might in fact serve a very good purpose. The fact that Jews don't eat pork or that Hindus don't kill cows might appear idiosyncratic or downright counter-adaptive. Religious dicta, however, suggests Harris, often turn out to be just the opposite and although shrouded in mysticism and magic can serve very basic needs of survival in a given community. So let's not dismiss the Dani as being a group of superstitious savages just yet. Their reasons for fighting might well be very sound. Equally the fact that they fight so frequently might not be such a disastrous affair either. Again we need to look at what happens – to examine in some detail the sequences and patterns of activity that make up a battle.

The challenge is issued. A small band of warriors have gone out in the early morning to the no-man's-land which separates their territory from that of a neighbouring tribe. Across this strip of land the invitation to battle is shouted. On the other side, the news is received in watch,towers and spread rapidly throughout the community. The challenge, it seems, is nearly always taken up. The excitement grows amongst the two sides. The only decision to be made now is whether to fight that same day or to wait until the next. Some important factors need to be considered here. Is there enough time to prepare – to dress up and eat the ritual sweet potatoes? More importantly, what is the weather like? Is it likely to rain? Rain can be a big problem. If you have spent most of the morning cleaning up your war head-dress plumes and carefully applying the coloured clay pigments to your face and body, you don't want it all ruined by a sudden downpour.

Assuming that the forecast is favourable, warriors from both sides will head for the pre-arranged battleground that same day. There is no hurry because the fighting can't start until both sides have signalled that they are ready. On the way, final tactics can be drawn up – strategies can be refined and contingency plans discussed. Some warriors will be stationed at various points some distance from the battleground itself. They are the reserve fighting groups. Usually they will do nothing unless the main attacking force sustains heavy losses and that doesn't happen very often. All the time, little magical ceremonies are being conducted. Old men sit by the fireside drawing trails through the ashes with sticks – a time-honoured method which allows the ghosts to see what is happening. Gardner sums up the final scene when both sides have arrived at the battle site:

By noon, most of the warriors have arrived and the various formations have taken more-or-less final positions. Some are armed with bows and arrows, some spears. The opposing armies are deployed so that between the most forward elements of each there lies a battle ground of perhaps five hundred yards. A mood of silent but excited expectation pervades all ranks. From this point on, the day will bring pleasures of the fight to several hundred on both sides, momentary terror for the handful who will feel the sudden pain of an enemy arrow, and, rarely, the unmentionable shock of death to someone who acts stupidly or clumsily.

There is a test of nerve here. The adrenalin races. Fear brings with it a special kind of watchfulness. Eventually one side sends forward a small advance group. They run forward, stop, run a bit more, and then follow nervously at a distance of some fifty paces from their rivals. They are caught in a classic bind between fear which pushes them back and aggressive pride which drives them on. The competing forces, for glory and self-enhancement on the one hand and for preservation of body and health on the other, lead to a jumping backward and forwards – the dance of indecision.

The rival group also advances. Some arrows will be fired. But these are crude arrows – they don't travel very far and they certainly don't travel very straight. To be hit by one of these arrows would be a great misfortune and little to do with the aim of the bowman. The reason for this is that the arrows have no flights on them. But why not? Dani culture is steeped in the knowledge and experience of birds in flight. Feathers and their properties are things which the New Guinea warrior understands completely. And yet he never uses these features to make his arrows fly true. Is this just plain ignorance – inability to use knowledge in a practical way? Or is it a very basic form of arms limitation? Perhaps the Dani warrior knows that the flights would mean that the arrows would kill. Perhaps this is not what arrows are for in the game he is playing.

The battle continues. Groups from either side sally back and forth. Eventually, with the preliminaries over, the main bodies clash. What happens now depends a lot on the prearranged tactics of each side and on the physical terrain of the battleground itself. Both sides try to split off small groups of rivals in order to ambush them. But the Dani know and fear the possibility of ambush. They take great pains to avoid such manoeuvres.

Sustained fighting rarely lasts for more than fifteen or twenty minutes at a time. The groups retreat to be replaced by other units.

If a warrior has thrown his spear he will, in any case, now be unarmed and vulnerable. He must retreat. And so it continues. Injuries will be sustained. Arrows and spearheads must be extracted from the bodies of one's fellows. A warrior limps with a broken-off arrow shaft sticking out of his buttock. It is removed simply by cutting it out, and the tip becomes the prized possession of the gallant warrior. It will hang proudly from the roof of his hut. Some elementary cleaning of the wound may fail to overcome infection, but the injury is unlikely to become a lasting one.

As the day wears on, the clashes become less frequent and sustained. Eventually, as both groups disperse and head for home, the whole business may simply become a slanging match. Rival warriors, now exhausted or limping, shout insults at each other across the battlefield before calling it a day. In Dani warfare a single death in battle is the cause of much remorse. It is an event which is sufficiently remarkable to warrant special rites and ceremonies. It calls for retribution – for further raids and the appeasement of yet more ghosts.

According to the anthropological sources, the death toll from a whole year of war and fighting is usually between ten and twenty warriors on each side – and this is in a culture where fighting and violence are integral parts of everyday living. In tribes where fighting provides a major focus of activity, where battles seem essential to the maintenance of their entire social fabric, more people, it has been claimed, die from the common cold than from the spears and arrows of rival warriors.

To talk of 'warfare' among the New Guinea plains warriors may be a little misleading. I've used the term so far only because that is the way in which anthropologists talk about hostile encounters between rival Dani tribes. But these battles are not like warfare in the sense we know it today. They are more like 'skirmishes' or 'raids'. There's nothing in the way of methodical and persistent infliction of death and destruction which has characterized recent wars in Western society. For the Dani warrior, preparation for battle is probably of more significance than the battle itself. And in this sense at least, he has much in common with the contemporary football rowdy. His 'wars' are directly comparable with terrace 'aggro'. He fights not because of some pressing political, economic or religious necessity. He fights because he is a fighter – a man for whom orderly aggressive rituals are as much a part of his life as weddings, funerals and paying homage to the ghosts of his ancestors.

Violence of this kind does not have the terrifying rationality associated with the struggle for survival in a world of scarcity and need. It arises as a solution to the problem of aggression – the thing which binds together a tribe because it is directed outwards. By channelling the competitive hostility outwards towards the tribe on the other side of the hill, social bonds within one's own group are reaffirmed and maintained. Demonstrations of character on the battlefield are converted into the tangible rewards offered by a community in which exhibitions of courage and solidarity are held in esteem. The warrior finds favour within the dominance hierarchy that is firmly sustained as part of the social fabric in which he lives out his life. The framework may seem illogical, but it works. And it copes more effectively with the aggression of men than the seemingly more civilized social structures we find in our own society. Aggression is recognized and managed – and that is a rational approach.

It would be a mistake to suggest that the Dani are completely typical in their management of battles and warfare. Anthropologists can sometimes mislead us a little. They can gloss over the uglier aspects of life in the cultures they study. It is also possible that even if the account of Dani violence is not distorted in this way, other tribes, even other tribes in New Guinea, might conduct their affairs of hostility and conflict in a rather different way. Most importantly, it may well be that where reasons for fighting are different the outcomes might also be different. In other words, patterns of violence might be directly related to the origins and causes of violence.

In the mountains of New Guinea, as opposed to the plains, a number of anthropologists have suggested, warfare is often a more deadly business. But here, in particular, battles seem instrumental in preserving a very vital balance in the ecological system on which mountain tribes depend for survival. Among the Maring, for example, battles against rival sub-groups are part of a very strict cycle of events involving the raising and killing of pigs, the burning and clearing of forest areas and the establishment of gardens. According to Marvin Harris, Maring wars are directly instrumental in driving neighbouring groups off their territory. The victors do not immediately occupy this territory but return to their own. The occupied territory lies fallow – the forest regenerates. Quite simply, warfare here ensures that clans who survive on the 'cut-and-burn' agricultural system do not cut-and-burn to such an extent that the whole population is endangered. Defeated Maring are forced to ally themselves with other clans until they can reconstitute themselves as a force and perhaps regain some of their lost gardens. And the cycle goes on – cutting the forest, rearing pigs, killing pigs, going to war, leaving the forest area to recover.

50

Marvin Harris likes these kinds of explanations. He insists that
there is a rational explanation for most things which at first seem
illogical and senseless. In a time when most social anthropologists
are tending to avoid the 'why does it happen' type of question he
stands as a man prepared to stick his neck out and handle very
thorny issues. His explanation of Maring warfare, which needs
much more space than is available to do it justice, seems reasonable.
But for our purposes there is a different point to be drawn out – the
fact that rather more people seem to get killed in Maring battles
than in those among the Dani. As the reasons for fighting become
more directly related to issues of survival – that is, as fighting
becomes instrumental – the possibilities for death and injury
increase proportionately. Put in more general terms, it's possible
that aggro, or ritual conflict resolution, requires a well-balanced
ecological system in which to operate. As the support system
becomes unbalanced – as the pressures of survival rise – the patterns
of violence change.

There is a snag, however, in this whole train of thought. If you ask
a Maring warrior why he is fighting he will give you reasons very
similar to those offered by the Dani. He will talk of unsettled feuds
and of ghosts needing to be avenged. He will not say that he is
fighting in order to preserve his culture's 'eco-system'. He knows
nothing of ecological requirements. And yet his fighting appears,
from the outside, to be geared to meet such requirements. Harris is
content to see this kind of affair as a safety valve – a 'cut-off'
mechanism which operates before the ratio of population to food
resources reaches a danger level. But how does such a valve work?
How are the requirements for survival translated into collective
action? Why do they take one form rather than another?

For a long time, answers to questions such as these have tended to
be rather simplistic. Some writers would have us believe that it can
all be explained in terms of instinct or genetically programmed
behaviour, which is the end-product of a process of natural selection. But this is not very helpful. It doesn't, for example, explain
why fights and conflict encounters take on particular forms. Animals such as lizards seem to have a behavioural repertoire consist-
ing largely of fixed action patterns. There's little variation to
account for and the instinct theories have obvious relevance here. In
the case of the Dani and the Maring, on the other hand, the picture
is much more complex.

The standard alternative to the genetic determinism package is
the explanation couched solely in terms of environmental influence.
According to this view, aggression and violence are both caused by

the social and environmental pressures which impinge on individuals. All behaviour is a function of what has been learned within a specific cultural system. That seems fair enough. But it still doesn't explain why the Maring fight in the way they do or why the Dani fight at all. Social forces are the things to study if we want to understand how a particular pattern of behaviour comes to be established. But if we wish to ask why it is there – what is its purpose or function – then we have to look elsewhere for an explanation.

Neither of the extremes in the nature/culture debate will provide us with much inspiration. In fact, this long-lasting controversy between the champions of genes and the liberal advocates of social conditioning has served only to distract us from the business of finding a more adequate and sensible explanation of human behaviour. It has arisen because one section of the academic world has tried to make the wrong connection between an examination of the animal world and the study of human social interaction. They have confused the levels of symbolic action I spoke of earlier. They have assumed that even the complex secondary levels of social conduct are explicable in terms of genetic endowment and preconditioned behaviour. In a similar manner other writers have assumed that even primary levels of symbolic activity are the result of learning and direct social conditioning.

As a consequence we might be led to suppose that the classic fixed stare of two rivals outside a dance hall is an aggressive display that results from peculiar child-rearing practices. Or we might be swayed by the idea that the idiosyncratic styles of verbal abuse on the soccer terraces are the result of a long history of selective breeding. Both views are equally misguided. But all is not lost. We can step out of this raging feud and seek another, more rational, line to pursue.

It is quite clear from animal studies that aggression, within a given species, is essential for survival. And we must be careful not to confuse it with hunting behaviour or predatory killing. It ensures that territories, food resources and sexual partners are distributed in a manner which allows for selective development. 'The survival of the fittest' has become a very misused slogan but that, whether we like it or not, has been the way of things in the animal world. At the same time, aggression has not excluded other basic requirements. Animals still rely on within-group cooperation, on affiliative relationships and, in many species, on a distinct pair-bond between the male and female reproducing pair. Parental responsibility and collective food sharing still have their place even in the law of the jungle. But it is aggression which keeps things in order. It leads to a steady organization of dominance and submission. A structure is imposed upon nature that makes possible the development of all those aspects of human life we find applaudable and sane. It is inconceivable that any species could evolve without this basic ingredient, without some force which could instil fear, produce a readiness to fight and a will to compete for the scarce resources. As we have already seen, the potentially destructive side of aggression became limited very early in the history of evolution. The requirements for survival having been established, the potentially non-adaptive aspects were trimmed through ritualization. And the result – a biologically rooted mechanism tailor-made to enable animals to make maximum use of an essentially hostile environment.

Since man evolved, one way or another, from other animal species it seems ludicrous to suppose that he alone managed to succeed without aggression – without needing the biologically based ordering process upon which other species have relied. To suppose that early *Homo erectus* suddenly stood up and threw away his genetic endowment is a quite untenable proposition. But what happened when man developed skills which other animals never managed to acquire? What happened when he began to use symbols and eventually created out of these a language? What happened when he was able to become removed, in a sense, from the primary level of action – to stand back and talk about it, discuss it and construct a new level of functioning? In a nutshell what happened when all of this allowed him to be a cultural animal?

Being a cultural animal brings new problems but also new solutions. The problems hinge around the erection and maintenance of a whole social fabric. Natural order is replaced by social order and although the social order owes much to the considerations of nature it is capable of going beyond such considerations. More importantly, it is capable of doing its primary task of regulating the needs and ambitions of a particular society in relation to the material resources available to it in a manner more direct than that of natural selection. There may even come a stage where genes are relatively redundant. Instead of requiring an aggressive gene, man may simply acquire a social order in which aggression is a culturally instilled process. Boys are taught to be warriors, to compete with their peers and to fight in certain prescribed ways. Because the primary needs of human societies remain, at one level, pretty much the same as other animal species, processes like aggression and affiliation are retained in the new order of things. But to ask whether this 'modern' aggression is now due to a gene for fighting or for cultural doctrines is to ask a non-question.

We may rightly suppose that the social order was orginally founded upon natural, and by implication, genetic orders. That we might take as a historical fact. But once culture has taken over the role of transmitting life-styles and social values there is no reason to suppose that the genetic imprint will remain. In fact there are many good reasons why it should not.

The Dani and the Maring are classed by Western anthropologists as 'primitives'. All that means, however, is that they have not reached the same level of technological sophistication as some other cultures in other parts of the world. But in evolutionary terms they are way up the ladder. They are miles past the point where man broke away from his primate cousins. And cultures in New Guinea are socially complex transmitters. They are powerful shapers and modifiers of human behaviour. Most importantly they continue to regulate the population, ensure the optimum tribal spacings and keep in balance the driving forces of competition and cooperation. They can do all this without the help of genes.

This really should not surprise us too much because the same kind of thing goes on in our own cultures, even at a basic level. Take population control for an example. At the present time we are getting very excited about there being too many people and not enough resources to adequately sustain them. As a result contraception, once thought of as wicked and sinful, suddenly becomes totally acceptable. Non-reproductive sexual practices, homosexuality in particular, rapidly become legalized. Even the moral censure recedes. Financial constraints are introduced which favour smaller rather than larger families. Within a very short space of time traditional attitudes are modified to accord with the new hazards faced by an expanding population.

How this happens need not be mysterious. Cultures allow for the exchange of experience. They allow for a range of modellings to take place. As situations change, the models change. The model of the large Victorian family which met admirably the needs of an expanding industrial society can be discarded in favour of the 2.2 children model – the model of a family which will fit into a standard size saloon car or the three-bedroomed semi-detached house. But whilst models change certain basic requirements remain. And certain basic aspects of the culture are also resistant to change. This is because they form part of what has been described as a positive feedback system. It is this system which gives us part of the key to man's continued aggressiveness. It helps us to understand why men continue to fight even when there appear to be few good reasons for them to do so.

Positive feedback systems are quite straightforward and sociologists have been using them to explain a number of social features for quite a time. Recently some anthropologists have also begun to make use of them. At its simplest a positive feedback loop is one that feeds on itself. It develops and maintains itself without much help from outside.

Electronic engineers and sound recordists experience the phenomenon all too frequently in the form of 'howl-round'. A sound picked up by a microphone is fed through an amplifier and subsequently to a loudspeaker. But if the microphone and loudspeaker are too near to each other, the microphone will pick up the output of the loudspeaker, feed it back into the amplifier, out to the speaker again *ad infinitum*. The effect is a painful high-pitched squeal that will persist until someone moves the microphone away or switches the system off. Once howl-round has started it will carry on even if the only sound being picked up is that which races around and around in the manner of a berserk perpetual motion machine.

For an example of a sociological application of this model we can return to soccer fans for a moment. A positive feedback explanation for alleged 'deviant' behaviour at football matches would run something like this. A few minor, initial disturbances at soccer grounds in the mid-1960s received attention from the media. A small group of established figures in society, posing in the role of 'moral entrepreneurs', condemned the disturbance as 'disgusting' and 'senseless'. This in turn led to increased attention and coverage being given to the things that football fans were doing – they suddenly became visible. Subjected to this attention, fans reacted. At least part of their reaction involved further acts classed as deviant by the rest of society. The media image of fans hardened. Attitudes of fans hardened. Deviant acts became more frequent. The guardians of morality became convinced that their original sense of outrage was fully justified. Further measures led to further reaction. Thus we witnessed a steady escalation levelling off into a persistent pattern of what is now the recurring 'horror' of football hooliganism.

Note that the positive feedback loop doesn't even attempt to explain the original minor deviance. It simply seeks to map out the manner in which major 'social problems' can be created out of such minor events once the cycle of action and reaction is firmly set in motion within a society. Now how does this help us to understand the continued presence of aggression and its expression in human societies?

Positive feedback loops work because factors operating in a society give rise to certain consequences. Clearly the presence of aggression in the early development of the human species had certain direct consequences. Once we had aggressive men everything else followed, bound up in a cycle which is virtually impossible to halt. A society which evolves from a state of nature in which men are obliged to compete aggressively with each other for scarce resources is one which is obliged to rear further aggressive males in order to maintain the *status quo*. But the act of rearing fierce males itself has consequences. Having aggressive males around makes hostility and conflict more probable. This in turn serves to reinforce the continuing need to rear aggressive male children. The cycle begins to pick up its own momentum. In the meantime the role of women in society starts to become fixed as well. Since aggression and dominance tend to be parcelled together in all animal life, and since it is the men who are being reared to be aggressive and not the women, the patterns of dominance and submission are also established in favour of men.

What keeps this whole cycle revolving even when the survival of a society may no longer directly depend upon its warrior strength is the fact that aggression has other beneficial consequences. In driving a competitive process it works towards at least one kind of progress. It ensures that the struggle against a harsh environment is not simply abandoned. Ironically it even serves as a foundation of cooperation – cooperation among men for whom aggression actually provides a bond, a social tie that yokes them together in a spirit of tough masculinity.

Along with this cycle man, like other animals, progressively ritualizes his aggression. When nothing is really at stake any longer, and when some aspects of the aggressive process are no longer particularly useful, ritualization ensures that the potentially harmful effects are kept well under social control. The positive aspects remain. The Dani flourish. They fight but that doesn't pose much of a problem.

This whole approach helps us to understand quite a lot. Even more usefully it helps us to discard some issues upon which anthropologists and ethologists have wasted a lot of time. One feature of positive feedback loops is that they achieve the amplifying and sustaining effects on the basis of only very minor biases or events. These original factors might even be minor fluctuations we would expect by chance. In the case of the original football hooliganism, this might well have been due to random happenings or what we might call a 'cultural mutation'. A few stories in the papers about fans fighting each other, a few TV cameras appearing at the grounds to take a closer look – it could all catch on extremely

56

quickly. In the case of aggression the story could be very similar. The original genetic inheritance from our evolutionary predecessors need not have been at all strong. A minor imbalance which endowed early man, and not early woman, with the edge on fierceness. It might even have arisen from marginal differences in the size and weight of members of the two sexes. But these differences have consequences and it is these consequences which fuel subsequent cycles of events of social adaptation.

Man then is not necessarily a victim of his genes. Rather he lives in social groups where a fundamental and basic level of aggression is perpetuated through a cultural mechanism that is alarmingly efficient. There may, of course, still be present in men an inherited predisposition toward aggressive expression. This inheritance, however, is unlikely to amount to more than a diffuse and undifferentiated force with little direct power. At most it would probably constitute a residual drive, a primal left-over from our ancestral heritage of the jungle. Some ethologists talk of a 'genetic suggestion', and that sounds about right. There is very little evidence to suggest that people display aggression now for the same reasons they did in the dawning of cultured civilization hundreds of thousands of years ago. All we have to assume is that man once was by nature aggressive. Today, his aggression is a cultural business.

This is not at all the same as arguing, like many naive sociologists and social psychologists, that aggression is simply a product of the immediate environment; that it has to do solely with the conditions in which children grow up, with families, schools, housing and relative poverty. While such factors will certainly influence the manner in which aggression is expressed, the feedback cycle which sustains the aggressive force itself operates independently from immediate social changes and shifts in the surface structure of societies. Aggression is transmitted at a much more basic level than this.

In the end, perhaps, there's little difference between a 'genetic suggestion' for aggression and aggression which is the product of a closed feedback system. After all, the implications are much the same whichever line we take. A genetic suggestion is just that and no more – it doesn't determine behaviour in any simple sense. Nor does a culturally transmitted process. Although, in both cases, aggression will be there waiting to be modified and used in a positive fashion, opportunities for management and control of this potentially dangerous force can arise whatever its origin. Because something has a genetic basis to it doesn't mean that it is immutable.

Equally the fact that something is a product of culture doesn't mean that it can radically be changed overnight. Only if we accept either, that genes rigidly determine behaviour, or that social engineering can radically alter all aspects of human action is there a need for further debate. Since neither view has much going for it, I'm content to let others engage in the heated exchange of rhetorics.

This kind of approach goes some way to explaining how and why aggression is kept in business. Societies would fall apart without it and nature and culture conspire together to prevent this happening. The same kind of reasoning can also give us some clues as to why it has always been the men, rather than women, who have fought each other and why it is that males have tended to come off the better in the dominance/submission stakes.

Marvin Harris's proposal for a positive feedback model was directed towards explaining patterns of dominance within cultures. I've adopted such a model to account for aggression, because dominance and aggression, as we've seen, are very much yoked together in the real world. There is, however, one rather unusual aspect of the cultural cycles I've been talking about. Women, many would claim, have been subjugated, dominated and generally repressed. But women have always had the means at their disposal to break the pattern of cultural transmission. It's they who have control over the birth and care of children. They could quite easily tip the population balance in favour of females through selective neglect of male babies and, with little effort, sabotage the development of masculinity by rewarding passive rather than aggressive qualities in those that survive.

The fact that women have never, in the entire history of our species, been able to grasp the power so freely available to them, and with it wrench dominance away from males, is an illustration of the bind in which a feedback loop places them. Once power is in the hands of men, women have little choice but to accept their lot – at least in a tribal society. Rearing passive males would often have led to a defenceless society – one easily annexed by a neighbouring community. Some kind of multilateral treaty would have been required – each signatory entering into a planned aggression-reduction pact. Sadly that's not the way tribal societies have ever conducted their affairs. And in any case, what would have happened to those positive elements of the aggression process – those which are involved in keeping up not only competitive rivalry but also those essential social bonds which owe their existence to competitiveness? Would they, too, have vanished in the wake of an early shift towards women's liberation or even female dominance? Or would the roles simply have been reversed – the myth of the Amazonian warriors becoming a reality?

The odds against any society being able to redress the inequalities in dominance and aggressivity have always been slim. One added problem has been that aggression has not only been parcelled up with straightforward dominance, it has also been very much linked to sexual exploitation. The football fan boasts of 'shagging' the local women, the Dani warrior wears his enormous penis sheath in battle, and the vanquished chimp presents his bum. In tribal societies, the most aggressive males have tended to be those more able to 'own' the most wives. This in turn meant that women were in short supply for the less physically powerful members. Those without wives were obliged to become even more competitive. Aggression leads to an unequal distribution of females. Scarcity of females leads to increased aggression. A new feedback loop operates within the larger feedback loop and the whole thing becomes even more difficult to stop. And if anyone doubts that a lack of women makes men aggressive they should read Napoleon Chagnon's account of *Yanamamö: The Fierce People*.

The Yanamamö, a tribe in South America, have the unenviable accolade of being the most violent people in the world. A quarter of the entire male population die as a result of combat. But even this is not sufficient to redress the imbalance which stays relatively fixed at twelve men for every ten women. The shortage of women is a constant source of deadly feuds, rape and the treatment of wives as negotiable commodities. The really strange thing about all this is that the shortage is created not by some biological quirk but by the systematic infanticide of female babies. Among the Yanamamö, as indeed among many other societies, sons are held in esteem whilst daughters are considered to be reproductive failures. They are either neglected or even killed with as little ceremony as that afforded to the runt of the pig litter. An interesting aspect of this female infanticide is that the Yanamamö seem to be unaware of the fact that they are killing more girls than boys. Despite the fact that male babies are considered more valuable, some still fall victim to the infanticide policy. According to Chagnon, the Yanamamö know only three numbers: one, two and more than two. As far as they are concerned more than two babies of each sex are killed and they are content to view their practice of infanticide as indiscriminate with respect to sex. They fail to realize that they are bringing the shortage of women upon themselves, and are then driven to extreme aggression in order to put things right.

A number of suggestions have been put forward to explain this odd state of affairs. Some centre around the fact that although the Yanamamö live surrounded by abundant and edible vegetation, there is a shortage of animal protein. Marvin Harris, in his typically circuitous but lucid style, suggests that Yanamamö men need to be extremely aggressive in order to be able to hold their own in the inter-tribal disputes over hunting territories. This might well be correct. From an extreme functionalist viewpoint one might say that the Yanamamö kill off their female infants in higher numbers than male infants because this leads adult males to become more aggressive. They will fight among themselves within their tribal communities but they will also raid other villages in order to steal their women. In the process they may be able to annex some hunting land, too. But it's the need for a woman more than real estate which is the immediate driving force.

This point is particularly stressed by Chagnon who, for reasons which are none too clear, seems to find the explanation in terms of animal protein scarcity quite unacceptable. He quotes one tribesman as saying: 'Even though we like meat, we like women a whole lot more.' But the fact that a shortage of women is the immediate precipitating cause of hostility doesn't mean that aggression can't have some other, less obvious, function. The fact that the imbalance in the sex ratios is artificially engineered in the first place means that we should perhaps look to factors outside of the mating business for a more cogent explanation of the Yanamamö's fierceness.

I raise the gory example of these South American Indians for two reasons. Firstly, it shows very clearly how the degree to which ritualization of aggression is successful depends very much on the material world in which groups of people find themselves. Total management of hostility, like the management of anything else for that matter, can only be achieved when the basic requirements for survival are adequately met. Once they are achieved, aggression remains to make sure that they are not lost – it maintains the *status quo* with little in the way of bloody side-effects.

In the case of the Yanamamö, ecological conditions demand a higher level of aggression than that which obtains in more fortunate societies. But the interesting point here is that although the fatality rate is alarmingly high, ritual solutions to aggressive conflict still figure very strongly in the Yanamamö culture. Wars between rival villages are common, but within communities there are very distinct patterns of aggression management. Chagnon, himself, makes this point very clearly:

War is only one form of violence in a graded series of aggressive activities. Indeed, some of the other forms of fighting, such as the formal chest-pounding duel, may even be considered the antithesis of war, for it provides an alternative to killing. Duels are formal and are regulated by stringent rules about proper ways to deliver and receive blows. Much of Yanamamö fighting is kept innocuous by these rules so that the concerned parties do not have to resort to drastic means to resolve their grievances. The three most innocuous forms of violence, chest pounding, side slapping, and club fights, permit the contestants to express their hostilities in such a way that they can continue to remain on relatively peaceful terms with each other after the contest is settled. Thus Yanamamö culture calls forth aggressive behaviour, but at the same time provides a regulated system in which the expressions of violence can be controlled.

The Yanamamö tribes of South America present something of a test-case for the thesis concerning aggression and its management that I have been proposing. The fact that here men die with such predictable regularity or, if they are more fortunate, grow up covered in scar tissue which results from the fact that physical combat is an almost daily routine, can be taken as a sad reminder of man's inherent brutality. But this is quite a wrong way of looking at the situation. We've seen that a high level of violence exists only because its instrumental value is required for survival. And even in this extreme case, ceremonial solutions evolve to ensure that non-instrumental violence is strictly contained. The Yanamamö need to go to war – they need aggression to keep up the struggle for a balanced diet – but within their tribal groups, social systems of conflict control ensure that deaths through violent combats, non-instrumental products of aggression, are kept to an insignificant level.

The second reason for raising this example is that it illustrates very dramatically the close association between aggression and sexual behaviour I mentioned earlier. Sex, in this context, is the pay-off of fierce dominance. Only men who are prepared to fight, to take up challenges and subdue rivals, are able to make it to the marital bed. The Yanamamö take things to the extreme, but even in this 'worst case' example we can see many aspects of social life which are very familiar. There still exists in our own society the notion that women are 'things' to be fought over. They are 'prizes' to be won through demonstrations of masculine assertiveness, toughness and an aggressive determination to dispose of rival suitors.

61

Tribal Rituals

Things, of course, have changed. The muscle-bound he-men – the Charles Atlas figures of today – are more likely to be found displayed in glossy magazines for male homosexuals than those aimed at women. Sheer physical toughness seems now to be much less highly prized. But competition among men for access to the most attractive women remains. Individual females are still seen as 'belonging' to particular men and attempts at stealing such properties can still result in a physical beating from the wronged owner. Women, of course, are right to be upset at this state of affairs. (Many, on the other hand, would also claim that this system suits them very nicely.) But let's consider what is involved in redressing the balance.

Sex is a reward for being aggressive. But the reward is for men only. The system could never work if women were equally involved in a competitive struggle for access to the most virile males. Once sex becomes associated with dominance and aggression, a social divide between males and females is inevitable. Because women are the prizes, their status is fixed in a very distinctive way. The dominance struggle is between men; females don't enter into it at this level, and thus their submissiveness is guaranteed by the cultural forces which are shaped through the actions of men. There is no way that this pattern can be radically altered by attempts to make men less aggressive. As we've seen, in a tribal context this would make a particular community vulnerable to the imperialist ambitions of its neighbours. But the strategy would also fail for another reason. The less aggressive males would fail in competition for wives. They would become fathers less often than their more dominant peers, and they would have less opportunity to influence the social development of subsequent generations.

This is a very great obstacle to change in any tribal society. The established patterns of dominance have been so unshakable that never in the history of our species has there ever been any sign of a society in which women held the reins of power. There is absolutely no evidence of truly matriarchal communities existing in any place at any time. It's true, some societies have been, or still are, matrilineal. Descent is traced through the mother's side of the family and not that of the father. But that doesn't mean that women have any real power or have any grip on dominance. Only in mythology has the female of our species ruled the roost. Myths, however, are a poor substitute for facts. Some liberationists continue to base their demands for sexual revolutions on references to Amazonians and other characters of pure fiction, but any real model for a feminist society is absent from our history.

It has to be said, of course, that our societies are very different from those of the allegedly 'primitive' tribes-people. Having moved away from a pattern of tribal living, opportunities for change in cultural trends and mores increase very significantly. But such opportunities pose problems of their own. Anatomy is not destiny even in the tribal villages. Similarly even the most ancient and traditional patterns of cultural organization do not dictate the destiny of people in modern societies. Changes, however, bring with them their own associated consequences. And to seek change, without regard for the implications of inevitably associated by-products of change, is not only dangerous – it can be completely counter-productive. One particular consequence of the changes which women's liberationists are currently demanding is an increase in aggression among females. There would seem to be no way of avoiding this. Dominance and aggression are in the same bag – you can't have one without the other. Having equal status with men in the dominance hierarchies which constitute the power structure of our society means entering into the domains of aggression which were once the prerogative of men. But whereas there have always existed for men informal institutions in which aggression can be channelled and managed, I see no signs of equivalent institutions emerging for women. In fact, women seem (and this is a dangerous generalization) to be totally disinterested in anything to do with aggression management. Many members of the Women's Liberation movement argue very forcibly that aggression has nothing to do with the philosophy to which they subscribe. They stress cooperation rather than competition and seek equality rather than a pattern of dominance and submission. And who could argue that such ideals are to be opposed? But the idealism leads to a dangerous naivety. It involves the assumption that gender-based differences in our societies can be eliminated, or even reversed, simply by collective subscription to notions of what ought and should be the normal pattern of interaction between men and women.

I must make it clear that I'm not in any way trying to argue against the fundamental tenets of the liberationist philosophy. Because imbalances of one sort or another have been present in human cultures since the dawning of civilization we should not idly sit back and accept an imagined inevitability. That is the mistake of the so-called neo-Darwinists, and one which I have no motivation to emulate. But when the pursuit of such a philosophy closes the door on a consideration of what is going to happen along the way, what are the additional consequences of emancipation, then one must express some alarm.

Tribal Rituals

The reasons for this alarm will, I hope, become clearer when we come to examine other social consequences of a shift away from tribal communities and when, in particular, we come to examine some of the changes in the expression of aggression in contemporary society. I raise the issue of female roles at this point only in connection with the close association that has existed in the past between aggression and non-erotic sexual behaviour. Today women may no longer be the prizes for which men fight. In this sense we are far more fortunate than the Yanamamö. But in the ritual expression of male conflict on the football terraces (and this is by no means a unique example) the management of aggression relies, at least in part, on quite distinctive gender differences within the society that surrounds it. The symbolic system works only because women are not involved. What would be the use of demasculinizing your opponent if the dominant figures within your group are female? Once women become involved in the everyday business of conflict and dominance, many of the traditional ritual solutions available to us become useless. The chimp presents his bottom as a token of submission only because of the existence of a female/submission equation in the chimp world. Dismissing a man's masculinity only does the social work of a stylized insult because masculinity and dominance are inextricably bound up with each other. Once these equations are broken, the business of aggro begins to rest on shaky foundations. In short, the breakdown of traditional patterns of dominance and gender-linked social roles will mean that new symbolic solutions to aggression will have to be found. The trouble here, though, is that we will have neither the model of animal nature nor the model of cultural tradition on which to build our social mechanisms of management and constraint.

The lesson to be drawn from the anthropological literature is quite simple. Each society faces a variety of material and ecological problems and devises quite specific social solutions with which to overcome them. On the surface, their institutions and cultural traditions may appear idiosyncratic and unique. But beneath the surface can be discovered universal processes – things which all men share and which are resistant to social engineering. They constitute the bedrock on which civilizations are erected. We can change the surface structure of our societies with startling rapidity, but the need to manage aggression remains. It doesn't go away because it is the force which plays a vital role in the achievement of change. Social revolutions do not come about as a result of a passive, idealist wish for things to be different. They happen because people fight for them. In this sense we can never escape from a fundamental irony of the human condition – a condition which we share with other animals. But animals get round the problem, the Dani flourish and even the Yanamamö survive. Their solutions may appear inappropriate in the context of technologically sophisticated modern societies. And indeed they are. Our own solutions must be shaped by different cultural moves. But if we look, even briefly, at the history of Western civilization, we find that fundamentally parallel systems for coping with the same phenomena have arisen, and have succeeded.

4

Aggro in History

School history textbooks invariably start with a chapter or two on the history of the Roman Empire. I remember vividly my standard issue text, its black cover chewed and dog-eared, with maps at the front, half-obscured by generations of bored first-formers, showing the geographical extent of Roman domination and influence in the years just after the birth of Christ. I can remember, too, the utter tedium of having to learn the names of successive emperors with difficult Latin names, their particular conquests and their contributions to this or that fundamental act of legislation. In Latin classes I was similarly unimpressed with the dry texts from Livy, Cicero and Tacitus. Rome was long burned and for me the subject was dead and closed. It was not until, many years later, I stood in the ruins of Pompeii and looked down the lava-scarred columns of the forum towards Vesuvius that classic history began to mean anything at all. Wandering past the bakery and the grindstones in Crooked Lane, peering in at the House of the Small Fountain and strolling around the garden of the House of Marcus Lucretius, I couldn't help but be struck by the familiarity of it all. Nearly two thousand years ago men and women went about their routine business of everyday living. People went shopping in the Street of Abundance, worrying about inflation and the price of bread, just as people today mutter on their way down to Woolworths. The still-legible graffiti on the walls reflected the timeless obsessions which are today given expression above the urinal in the local pub. Only the brothel and heated baths reminded me that this was another country and a different millennium. But why hadn't the history books conveyed this sense of familiarity and closeness? As I stood in the circle of the amphitheatre, still not completely excavated, I felt at home, I could have lived here.

My experience, I am sure, is not unique. The neglect of history and ancient civilizations is something which continues to bedevil work in virtually all areas of the social sciences. Today's social

66

problems are somehow removed from those of the past. We come to view them as novel and special, the products of contemporary factors that have little to do with the problems of previous eras. Our lives are our own, and the fact that they have probably changed little since the days of Pompeii is something which rarely occurs to us.

Aggro, though, is far from being a novel creation of the post-war youth culture. It has parallels, as we have seen, in the animal world which are so striking that we are inescapably drawn to the conclusion that aggro owes, at least at one level, something to evolution. Ritual fighting among the so-called primitive tribes of the New Guinea plains, and even the South American forests, also suggests that aggro is very much part of a basic human way of life. It seems inconceivable that aggro has been anything other than a major social phenomenon throughout the history of man. Every generation in all societies faces the same kinds of problems that their ancestors faced. Governments may come and go and entire empires rise and fall within a space of time that represents only the briefest interval on the evolutionary time-scale. The requirements for survival, both physical and social, change little. The obstacles to human fulfilment, even in an age of machines and undreamed-of powers, are basically unaltered. To survive and flourish we compete with the limitations of the material world. And to exist as social animals, we both compete and cooperate with each other.

And so to history. Where has aggro been? Where were the football hooligans and Dani warriors of yesterday and the days before that? What were bovver boys up to in the days of long since fallen empires?

In the days of the early Roman emperors, from the first century AD onwards, the circus provided the main focus of entertainment. Inside the hippodromes and the stadia, which were often built in the middle of cities and large communities, raced the charioteers – the colourful legends in their own times. Chariot racing commanded great skill, courage and fast horses. Like sport today, both the riders and their equipment were big business and because of the circus' great appeal to the *populus romanus*, a profitable entertainment industry flourished. The *Circus Maximus* in Rome, for example, was enlarged, on the instructions of Nero, to accommodate 200,000 spectators – twice the number Wembley or even the Houston Astradome will hold. With the industry flourished groups of rival spectators who formed the early circus factions. On the race track, charioteers rode in the colours of their particular faction – red, white, blue or green. Of these, the Blues and Greens had come to

67

dominate the field. In doing so, the rivalry between them became more intense.

In a letter written at the end of the first century AD, Pliny the Younger gives us an intellectual's personal account of the circus. His attitude both to the games themselves and to the spectators might sound very familiar.

> I have spent the past few days very pleasantly and restfully among my books and papers. You may wonder how that was possible in Rome. Well, the games in the Circus Maximus were on, and I'm not the least bit interested in that kind of show. There's nothing new, no variety, nothing for which once is not enough. This makes me all the more surprised that so many thousands of grown men are prepared to see over and over again in such childish fashion galloping horses and men driving the chariots. If they were attracted by the horses' speed or the drivers' skill, there might be some sense in it. But as it is, they merely support a piece of cloth; that is what they follow, and if two colours were changed over in the middle of the actual race their support and allegiance would change too and they would immediately desert the drivers and horses they recognize from their seats and whose names they shout.
>
> Fancy such influence and power wielded by one worthless shirt, not merely among the common crowd, which is more worthless even than that, but even among some men of taste. When I see this sort of person so insatiably fond of a sport which is so empty, meaningless and repetitive, I must admit to a feeling of pleasure that the pleasure is not for me. So for the past week I have readily spent my idle hours in writing while others have been wasting theirs in the most idle pursuits.
>
> (*Letters*, Book IX, 6)

Pliny sounds very much like some of the pedantic arbiters of taste we find today – indeed, in his contemptuous dismissal of the mass leisure of his time, he resembles closely a few academics I know who think that football is a game only for those with their brains in their feet. Nonetheless Pliny's account highlights very clearly the passions and factional interests that could be aroused even by 'worthless shirts' of a particular colour.

Along with the spectacle of chariot racing, the theatre also occupied an important position in the Roman's social calendar. Pantomime was his particular favourite. The theatre, however, was a noisy and often turbulent affair. You didn't go simply to listen and be entertained. You went to become involved in the whole business

68

– to catcall and boo and to generally let off steam. In Pompeii, in AD 59, disturbances reached such a level that the amphitheatre was actually closed for ten years by the Senate after a battle between local residents and visiting Nucerians who came to enjoy a performance.

So when, in the fourth century as the Byzantine era dawned, the theatre-goers joined up with the circus factions a predictable sense of alarm and outrage spread throughout the Empire. The circus factions in the past had displayed intense rivalry towards one another. But there had been little in the way of serious trouble. With the added membership, however, things began to change. The young theatre rowdies, finding life in the amphitheatres and forums not quite so easy as it once was, and finding themselves the subject of censure wherever they went, saw the circus with its ready-made social groupings as an obvious opportunity for new excitement. And so appeared the new Blues and the new Greens; the truly classical hooligans. Now they were not just a Roman phenomenon. Their influence had spread to Constantinople and the heart of the Byzantine Empire.

The history of the Blues and Greens is, of course, rather more complex than this. The early factions played quite definite, although sometimes exaggerated, roles in the everyday political and social affairs of Roman communities. But from the fourth century onwards, factions were essentially similar to present-day groups of rival bovver boys. They wore their colours proudly, they championed their favourites through fortunes good and bad, and they remained loyal even in the face of opposition and defeat. The parallels don't end here. Like today's rowdies, their activities centred around aggro and fights, the details of which are uncannily similar to those outlined at the beginning of this book.

It all happened well over a thousand years ago of course. We can't examine the factions at first hand any more – we can't stand and watch what happened. But we can piece together from contemporary sources a reasonable picture of life on the terraces of the first few centuries after Christ. We can also make use of material collected, in a painstaking manner, by Professor Alan Cameron in *Circus Factions: Blues and Greens at Rome and Byzantium.*

Chariot racing had become such a central feature of life in the early Byzantine era that control over the events had been taken away from private enterprise and was now the responsibility of the local senate. The Blues and Greens, however, remained the driving force and were primarily responsible for initiating the chanting and cheering which accompanied every race. They occupied the best positions in the stadium from which to achieve this and the words of the chants sum up the kind of atmosphere which must have been present. For example:

Burn here, burn there,
Not a green anywhere.

Set alight, set alight,
Not a blue in sight.

Something of their true impact is lost in translation. But one can readily imagine a body of Chelsea or Manchester United fans charging into their rivals' End and chanting the same lines (with a little colour correction). In fact the Blue and Green chants quoted here occurred in just these circumstances. Ends existed in Roman and Byzantine arenas in just the same way as they figure prominently in football grounds. Invasion of the opposition's territory was a regular feature according to contemporary accounts of 'riots'. Such territorial ambitions also spread outside of the grounds.

Unlike today, each major town had its share of both the Green and the Blue fans. Most British towns usually have only one distinct 'tribe' of supporters, and so, except for Saturdays, the general public is spared a continual war being waged on its doorstep. But in Rome and Byzantium things, in this respect, were rather different. Greens and Blues even had areas of cities marked out as their own pieces of turf, rather like the 1950s gangs of American cities. Opportunities for aggro were thus more frequent. But it usually took an actual chariot event to spark off anything more than a few minor feuds. It was the passions of fanatical and sycophantic members of the factions, aroused by the colourful spectacle of the races, that spilled out of the grandstand and into the neighbouring streets.

One other centre for strife and fighting between the Blues and Greens existed around the rival club houses and stables which usually adjoined the hippodrome itself. It was here that the Byzantine bovver boys met as social groups in an atmosphere of something like a modern youth club. Since the club houses were often quite close to each other minor vandalism was a fairly frequent occurrence, and petty thieving from the rival's club was also common.

To some extent the scene must have been quite similar to that which exists in present-day Siena. Each year the magnificent shell-shaped Piazzo del Campo becomes an arena for one of the most magnificent horse races in Europe – the Palio. Each horse in the race is owned by groups of people who constitute the Contrade, the rival bands who each have their own stables and bars in the small streets leading off the square. Each Contrada is a tightly knit social unit, its members all usually living within a small, well-defined area. Such groups jealously guard their horses and the ceremonial flags and drapes which are brought out to produce the magnificent sight on the twice yearly race days. Quarrelling among rival Contrade is not exactly unknown. Doping of another group's best horse is also not unprecedented. The Palio and the ceremonies associated with it have, of course, been 'cleaned up' in recent years. There is still widespread bribery of riders and a general air of crooked dealing surrounding the whole affair. But there are few brawls between rival groups – at least not in public. That is the price you pay for becoming a tourist attraction.

The Palio of Siena is much more recent than the Byzantine circus factions. It has its origins in the fourteenth-century ceremonies of medieval Tuscany, rather than in the sports of the Romans who, having stolen the city from the Etruscans in the time of Augustus, were forced to relinquish control of it as the influence of the Western Empire eventually dwindled away. But strolling around the narrow streets and peering cautiously into the small bars with the name of the Contrada and its colours above the door, you can get some sense of what it must have been like 1500 years ago as the Byzantine era gained momentum and the Blues and Greens sat in their club houses discussing over jugs of wine the tactics to be employed to humiliate their long-standing rivals.

Distinctive forms of dress are things always associated with ceremonial forms of fighting. The whole business of dressing up, posing in the right gear, is itself part and parcel of the ritual in which one group of men and boys tries to establish dominance over another. At the most basic level it serves clearly to mark out who are your friends and who are your enemies. The Greens and Blues, of course, dressed in the colours of their faction. Identification was immediate. There was more to it than this, however. One aspect of the faction dress was particularly interesting – the sleeves of the tunics that they wore. Football fans of the current age wear scarves in the colour of their team, not as you might expect, around the neck, but around the wrist, a part of the body where they can't possibly serve the function for which scarves were designed. Having a scarf tied in this way serves a very different purpose. As hands rise in collective cheering and gesturing the colours of the team follow like flags in lofty salute. The wide sleeves of the factions would have served exactly the same purpose – as emblems of allegiance clearly visible to all in the hippodrome.

Flags themselves are something which also figure at British football matches, although they are most commonly seen at the big Cup Final games in Wembley Stadium. This practice is something which was copied from Italian fans who continue to use them more extensively. The flags, in the team colours, and with the club insignia on them, are paraded proudly by members of the semi-official supporters' clubs in a style very similar to that at the Palio. Did the Contrade pick up the habit from the circus factions? Are the Celtic and Rangers fans in Glasgow waving, respectively, green and blue flags and banners, engaging in a bit of symbolic behaviour that has been handed down from the sports fans of classical times? The route might seem a little circuitous, but the parallels are uncanny.

The rowdyism and riots of Byzantine factions had little direct political motivation or purpose. According to Alan Cameron, at least, those who have suggested that the Blues and Greens were champions of one or other vested interest, or a particular socioeconomic stratum within their society, are quite wrong. They were fans and we should ascribe no more political ambition to them than to the average devotee of a league football club. The circus was their life. If you were a Blue you lived to see your particular brand of charioteers win every race. And you also lived to put down, at every opportunity, anybody who dared to insult your group by applauding the Greens. The factions were not in opposition to the government of the day, nor were they revolutionary or resistance groups. In fact, they were probably as conservative as the average British soccer fan who tends to be more interested in who is going to win the F.A. Cup than the next general election.

The riots of the factions received a predictably bad press. The scribes and pundits and high-minded scholars such as Pliny poured forth papyrus diatribes which would not look out of place in the *News of the World*. Outrage was widespread. The general consensus was that it was pointless, futile and stupid. It was not like the gallant fighting of centurions whose violence had some higher ideal attached to it, and whose actions were directed at achieving something that was essential or at least useful. All the factions cared about were their colours, the things that gave them identity in a bureaucratic society. Elders were at a loss to see how this could possibly contribute to the common good.

Of the actual events which took place during the riots themselves the record is confused. Bearing in mind how distorted and contradictory are present-day accounts of similar disturbances, this is not surprising. But one thing does seem fairly clear. The Blues and Greens were not engaged in the business of murder or mutual assassination. There are very few reliable records of deaths arising as a result of mass confrontations between the factions. There were other kinds of riots going on during the same period. There were violent political disturbances, riots sparked off by simple things like the price of corn, and bloody battles in the streets between rival religious organizations. In these, injuries were often severe and extensive. They were nothing, however, to do with the Blues and Greens. Theirs was an altogether different kind of fight.

Damage to property, rather than serious injury, was the most characteristic aspect of a factional riot. The Greens, in particular, seemed very fond of setting fire to things. In a property conscious society it was this that aroused so much indignation amongst the decent, right-thinking bourgeoisie. The actual extent of this vandalism seems unrecorded. If, however, Byzantine society was at all like our own, it would not have taken a great deal to spark off the whole amplification process which magnifies the significance of any such activity to the point where a whole new reality is created. Even so, there were at least some liberal-minded officials in Constantinople who, whilst decrying the behaviour of the factions, recognized the positive function that the circus played. It was seen as a safety valve. Young men could let off steam and act out their striving towards dominance and manhood. It is reasonable to assume that death and destruction must have been limited to a level that made such official strategies tolerable. Whilst the circus remained, aggression and the expression of factional hostility could be contained. People didn't like it but they probably enjoyed complaining about it. Whilst the Blues and Greens directed their energies at each other they remained little of a threat to the *status quo*. Economic and social worries could come and go, but the factions would rather engage in structured rumbles at the race track than storm the seats of power or attack senators in their villas.

The circus factions, then, stand out as very obvious antecedents of contemporary football hooligans and bovver boys. Alan Cameron is also quick to see the immediate parallels.

It is clear enough from the evidence . . . that there *is* a direct connection between the games and faction misbehaviour just as there is between the football stadium and soccer hooliganism today. But in neither case is the violence to be explained *solely* in terms of the excitement generated by the dancers or footballers. Other factors are certainly involved. In both cases there is undoubtedly a ritual element. . . . The games can serve as a field where the youth who leads an otherwise ordinary and unexciting life can prove himself a man by fighting and destroying . . . for an hour or two he can be an object of fear to all those who cross his path. The problems and anxieties that dog his everyday life will be dissipated in the excitement.

Without intending any disrespect at all to Cameron, when Professors of Latin are so struck by the function of ancient conflicts such as these, when they cannot help but see their ritualistic nature, it is time we all woke up to the fact that aggro has a very long pedigree.

Not all antecedents of aggro have been quite so obvious or spectacular as the feuds between rival circus factions. And it's because of the fact that aggro varies in its variability from society to society, and generation to generation, that some people see it as being wholly a function of special social circumstances. It comes and goes, they suggest, depending on prevailing trends and the mores of a particular culture. But just because the business of ceremonial conflict resolution doesn't always take the form of elaborate and colourful spectacles, it doesn't mean that the essential elements which constitute aggro are absent. The fundamental subscription, by males, to an orderly framework in which rivalries can be safely settled appears in more subtle but no less effective forms in whatever period of history we care to examine. It may even be that some aspects of war itself were once essentially ritual affairs.

To suggest that modern warfare has anything in common with aggro would be pretty ridiculous. Pomp and ceremony remain in the barracks drill squares but that is about all. In this age of nuclear overkill wars go on. But since the dawn of the twentieth century, at least, they have become totally unlike the gentlemanly affairs that characterized battle between rival armies in times past. Technology has ruined it all. Today we have a push-button bull's-eye battle. No longer do you need to see the whites of your enemy's eyes. You don't need to see him at all. You watch your electronic screen, press a button, and he is blown to oblivion with chilling certainty. He is 'mopped up' – the area is 'neutralized'. A new, frightening, symbolic rhetoric emerges to mask the grim and deadly reality of it all.

For the moment I want to leave, but not ignore, the other side of the violent coin. I come to killing after aggro because I believe that it is only when we have seen that violence is not just a one-dimensional and complete catastrophe that an analysis of why men kill each other can be properly made. It is when we have teased out aggro from today's violence and from the riots of history, when we have got to grips with the 'little bit of violence never hurt anyone' that we can steel ourselves for the much more grim task of understanding atrocity and genocide.

One writer who has done more than most to point out the essentially ritual nature of certain kinds of warfare in earlier times in our history is the anthropologist, Robin Fox. Although I feel he is quite wrong in suggesting that ritual solutions to man's aggressiveness are really no longer possible in the complex and technologically advanced urban societies of the present day, he does us a good service in pointing out the almost absurd constraints present in traditional battles. Medieval knights, it seems, took things to elaborate extremes. The life of the European knight of the Middle Ages was one which revolved around rigidly held concepts of chivalry, honour and gallantry. And the way in which he fought very much reflected the social codes.

> War was not about killing all those peasants – one could do that anytime – war was about knights. The lances that they used were ridiculous. As people who set up tournaments and try to use them know, it was terribly difficult to manoeuvre a lance, to do anything but simply knock someone off this horse. It was terribly hard to damage somebody protected by a ton of armour around him, and of course when he fell he could not move and so was easily captured. The whole thing was almost absurdly designed to this end.
>
> ('The Inherent Rules of Violence')

We mustn't, however, get too carried away with this image of colour and ceremony. It is quite clear that the tournaments of the knights were very ritual affairs. But only when they fought among themselves. In these affairs of rivalry and honour, enacted by young men eager to make their mark and win fair ladies, all was constrained and quite amicable. But sadly, despite what Fox seems to think, war, rather than jousts and tournaments, did involve killing a lot of peasants. Michael Howard, in his delightfully concise book *War in European History*, makes the point that:

> Much of the 'Middle-Ages' is still seen through the distorting lenses of fifteenth century legend, which cast upon the whole world of 'chivalry' a golden fictitious glamour, a sunset glow from a consciously disappearing society.

A quite vital distinction has to be made here between 'private' and 'public' wars. Private wars were waged between the knights of one feudal landowner and the knights belonging to a rival fiefdom. Such *guerre couverte* was conducted in a manner calculated to cause little damage to the community in general and, since it centred around encounters between men wedded to the philosophy of a chaste and honourable lifestyle, bloody murders were infrequent. Public wars, on the other hand, were waged between the massed armies of imperialist princes and here there were far fewer constraints. Killing peasants in the fields or monks in their abbeys was still considered 'not done', but often an invading army would find some excuse to carry out quite savage reprisals on the civilian population. In siege warfare, in particular, butchery was very often sanctioned and few people were afforded any immunity at all.

The point here is that the social fighting among knights themselves was very much like the aggro of today. They were evenly matched and all subscribed to the same set of ideals and values. They were all bound within the same social framework and accepted equally its restrictions on their activities. But when the conflict spilled outside of this framework, when the objects of their attacks were no longer other knights but ragged foot soldiers of very much inferior social positions, the ritual solution was much less in evidence. Codes of conduct existed, but like the Geneva Convention of today these rules were far from being the preservers of life and limb we might have wished for.

Warfare, even in the Middle Ages, begins to stretch aggro to its limits and often beyond. It involved armies of men far more numerous than that of a tribe. And there comes a point where killing can no longer be limited within the constraints of symbolic frameworks. The ritual solution runs out of steam because the direct face-to-face communication that it relies on is thwarted by the sheer numbers of people involved. The really remarkable thing is that the ceremonial constraints should have extended as far as they did – that the codes of honour and even courtesy should have remained in action even when battles had become rather more than a matter of striving for dominance and masculine pride. That 'gentlemen's agreements' could still be held as binding in the otherwise bloody business of annexing land or defending one's castle is something which is quite astonishing.

When wars became rather different from the inter-tribal conflicts which were so characteristic in man's earlier periods of development, the ritual processes which emerged to control small group social encounters began to run out of effectiveness. They still shaped, to some extent, conduct on the battlefield, but they could no longer limit the killing to such a significant extent. But they can go on working in the everyday lives of young men as effectively as they always have done. And the social constraints don't always need to involve dramatic costumes or theatre-like settings. Whilst aggro becomes highly visible in the Byzantine hippodrome or the British football ground, or the tournaments of the knights, it also has a much less spectacular history. Consider this account of fighting in the streets of London provided by a Huguenot refugee who arrived in England in 1685:

> If two little boys quarrel in the street, the passengers stop, make a ring around them in a moment, and set them against one another, that they may come to fisticuffs . . . during the fight the ring of bystanders encourages the combatants with great delight of heart, and never parts them while they fight according to the rules. And these bystanders are not only other boys, porters, and rabble, but all sorts of men of fashion, some thrusting by the mob that they may see plainly. . . . The fathers and mothers of the boys let them fight on as well as the rest, and hearten him that gives the ground or has the worst. These combats are less frequent among grown men than children, but they are not rare. If a coachman has a dispute about his fare with the gentleman that has hired him, and the gentleman offers to fight him to decide the quarrel, the coachman consents with all his heart. The gentleman pulls off his sword, lays it in some shop with his cane, gloves and cravat, and boxes in the same manner as I have described above. . . . I once saw the late Duke of Grafton at fisticuffs in the open street, with such a fellow, whom he lambed most horribly. In France we punish such rascals with our cane, and sometimes with the flat of the sword; but in England this is never practised. They use neither sword nor stick against a man that is unarmed, and if an unfortunate stranger . . . should draw his sword upon one who has none, he'd have a hundred people upon him in a moment, that would, perhaps lay him so flat that he would hardly ever get up again until the Resurrection.

I have provided quite a long extract here because its author, Misson de Valbourg, provides us with a very lucid account of plain, simple and straightforward seventeenth-century aggro. He reveals a whole set of social attitudes which recognized the fact that young men would, not infrequently, enter into aggressive disputes with each other. They also reflected a simple, but seemingly effective, rule framework which rendered the whole business manageable and acceptable. So long as men fought fairly and didn't make use of

77

more effective tools at their disposal, social censure was held back. Nobody interfered, the dispute was settled and the antagonists went home with nothing more than a few bruises. Using a weapon against an unarmed man – a very efficient way of dealing with any rival – was not only frowned upon, it also made the perpetrator liable to even more deadly retribution. The most striking aspect about these fights is that the community in general, from the porter to the man of fashion, was quite prepared to tolerate, even encourage, a kind of violence which today sends people into paroxysms of outrage. The notion of fisticuffs and the concept of the 'fair fight' have been very pervasive in modern history. In Britain and other countries, unarmed combat between men had an aura of dignity and decorum about it, and to some extent this exists today. Pub fights or brawls in the street are not exactly governed by the Queensberry rules, but the concept of the 'dirty' punch or the 'unfair' blow to an 'illegal' part of your opponent's body is still very often present. The phrase 'below the belt' has even found a permanent place in the English language as an indication of a socially unacceptable way of scoring a point over somebody else. On the other hand, though, we as a society seem far less content to leave fisticuffs alone. Today a 'fair fight' is often bemoaned as being 'playground violence', or 'football violence' or 'street violence' or simply 'senseless violence'. Policemen feel it their duty to intervene, social workers are brought into the act to work out why it happens, schoolteachers have nervous breakdowns and the newspapers have a field day.

In Misson de Valbourg's day folk were far less upset by it all. Even in societies where the armed duel was a standard method of settling matters of honour, the public, with only a few notable exceptions, showed little concern. If two men, with their seconds standing by, wanted to fence with each other or to blow themselves apart with pistols, that was their affair. Old scores had to be settled somehow. Indeed a man was not a man unless he was prepared to fight for his principles or put down a rival who seriously threatened his reputation and character. Innocent bystanders, and there would have been few of these at the dawn-rise ceremony, were not harmed. And despite the popular myths, duels were seldom fights to the death. The pistols they used were very inaccurate and clumsy affairs, and in sword fencing the aim of the exercise was not to slash your opponent to pieces, but skilfully and gracefully to out-manoeuvre him and force him to retreat. Gory Errol Flynn figures were few and far between. However, as Knipe and Maclay point out in *The Dominant Man*, noble duellists did get killed. In fact, in the space of time between 1589 and 1608 some 8000 were killed in France alone. But, 'Since the great majority of such affairs of honour were *not* fatal, these figures do not give a true reflection of the number of duels actually fought in France at that time.'

Duelling among the French aristocracy was an almost daily ritual and there can have been scarcely a man of nobility who had never once been forced to draw his sword or to get out his brace of pistols. The weaponry made it much more hazardous than the fist fight, which was the Englishman's traditional way of doing things, but the social codes, with their now familiar restraining function, limited the prestigious disputes to manageable proportions.

French duellists were similar to contemporary aggro boys in that they fought each other on the slimmest of pretexts. In pubs and dance-halls the inadvertent glance is seized upon as an offensive stare; as a challenge and a reason to engage in a fight. Similarly to the French nobility the most trivial of remarks could be taken as a damaging slight to one's honour. Some titled men, in fact, made a whole career out of duelling, inviting any man with a reputation for fencing or shooting to prove his worth and his skill there and then. This, however, was taking things a bit far and Louis XIII was obliged to have one of these career duellists, the Comte de Bouteville, executed in order to maintain a more easy balance to the whole masculine rivalry issue. It was de Bouteville, of course, who when asked by the Bishop who attended his execution, 'Are you still thinking of your life?' replied, 'I am only thinking of my moustachios – the finest in France.' Male chauvinist vanity was preserved to the bitter end.

Duels of honour spread from France to Britain in the seventeenth century as a result more of public opinion than chivalric notions on the part of the aristocracy. It never reached the epidemic proportions that it had done in France, but it nonetheless came to be a significant institution through which aggrieved and injured men of noble distinction could repair damage to their names and reputations. Again the whole duelling business was conducted within a very rigid framework of fixed rules and etiquette. Like the earlier Middle Ages duels of chivalry, where knights fought knights in ridiculously encumbered splendour, earls, dukes and gentlemen preferred that certain issues of conflict be settled by man to man confrontation than through the arbitration of external agencies. 'Satisfaction' was what they required, and that was not something you got by going to law.

It has to be remembered, of course, that duelling arose because of a lack of law and the agencies to enforce it. The original judicial

79

duels were between the man accused of an offence and his principal accuser, although the duels themselves were often fought by professional proxies. Thus if you wanted to accuse a man of murdering your father, then you might find that it was not he who was hanged but yourself because of the failings of your proxy. However, even when the rule of law developed to an extent where this unnecessarily arbitrary system was made redundant, duelling continued. It was cloaked in a new mantle and, most importantly, it did not have killing as its prime objective.

Like 'fisticuffs', the duel of honour was a distinctive brand of aggro in that it was fought by two individuals rather than by groups of men. But they fought within the bounds prescribed by a much wider set of social conventions. They recognized each other as belonging to the same order within society and as sharing the same basic tenets and principles of a common philosophy. Although the duel was a personal affair of pride and integrity, fought between the aggrieved and the man who had slighted him, the fight still had to be conducted in front of gentlemen who could bear witness to the following of rigid protocols. Instead of engaging in frenzied attacks in the heat of passionate rage, men were obliged to cool their tempers and enact a lengthy ritual of issuing and accepting cartels before the fight could begin. As a result, even the fiercest of protagonists would often settle for a token exchange of fire and an apology, his heart no longer being in the business of mortal retribution. Conflicts were resolved not so much at ten paces on the damp morning grass but, almost by default, in the tedious ritual preparations.

Duels in Britain, even more so than those in France, were fatal in only a minority of cases. The rituals never reached the stage where they were totally efficient in sparing life, but as a means of settling feuds or threats to integrity, they didn't do a bad job. This was not the case, however, in America.

Robert Baldick, in his book *The Duel*, draws upon sources which provide for a very useful contrast between the ritualized duel in Europe and the rather different brand of armed conflict in which American men engaged. He quotes, for example, Alexis de Tocqueville who, in 1831, commented:

> In Europe one hardly ever fights a duel except in order to say that one has done so; the offence is generally a sort of moral stain which one wishes to wash away, and which most often is washed away at little expense. In America one only fights to kill; one fights because one sees no hope of getting one's

adversary condemned to death. There are very few duels, but they almost always end fatally. (*The Duel*)

Duelling, if that is the word for it, spread to America rather later than it became a regular feature of European upper-class circles. But the rules and values didn't arrive with it. Instead the business became more akin to what one commentator called 'shooting on sight' than a gentlemanly ceremony. The image of men in ten-gallon hats, facing each other down dusty streets – the vision of lusty masculinity so loved by Hollywood film producers – is probably over-romantic. Men shot their rivals without any regard for the niceties of elaborate codes of conduct. They shot them because they wanted them dead and because the rule of law was often almost non-existent. A duel in which nobody was killed was likely to be described as 'poor shooting' rather than a laudable sparing of life. Only when men put aside their guns and, in true John Wayne style, slugged it out together in front of the saloon, was there any prospect of settling disputes without serious bloodshed. The trouble is that, in the frenzy of frontier pioneering, the gun was the only thing which really settled anything.

Looking for aggro in American history is like looking for the proverbial needle in an equally proverbial haystack. Even today, Americans find the concept difficult to handle. They have little experience of it and little in their past to give them any idea of the principles on which it is based. All of which might go some way towards explaining why the USA is in such a violent mess. It may be that in Britain folk are getting out of the habit of 'old-fashioned' violence which, relatively, hurts less than it might. Americans, on the other hand, never acquired the habit in the first place. The manner in which their nation was carved out by a highly mixed bunch of *émigré* settlers and frontiersmen may have had a lot to do with this fact. Joe Frantz, author of *The American Cowboy*, summed up the heritage of the modern USA in an article called 'The Frontier Tradition: An Invitation to Violence':

> The fact that back East, which meant ten miles behind the cutting edge of civilization all the way to the more sophisticated capitals of Europe, men were daily facing monumental problems of planning, and sometimes even of surviving, meant nothing to the frontiersman. Nothing in the frontiersman's way of life gave him any sympathy for the man who made his decisions on paper or in the vacuum of an office or stall. Decision was made on the spot, face to face. The questions were simple; the solutions equally simple. Today that heritage

81

of the frontier continues in remote areas. The subtleties of law and order escape the isolated mountain man, for instance, whether he be in Wyoming or in Eastern Kentucky. If a man does wrong, you chastise him. . . .

One of the acceptable forms is murder, which means that lesser violence visited upon the offending person is even more acceptable. Such behaviour has the advantage of being swift and certain, without the agony of deciding what is comparatively just and without the expense of trials and jails and sociologists and welfare workers.

Early Americans were faced with big problems. The very nature of their task demanded a high level of aggression – aggression aimed at manipulating a wild and often cruel environment into a supportive environment. But they lacked a culture on which to fall back and in which to achieve some orderly mechanism for resolving inevitable conflicts. Pioneering was a greedy business, and without shared systems of managing the interpersonal consequences, things were bound to be pretty bloody. The makeshift response to violence within the early communities was to throw up various bands of vigilantes who were charged with the unenviable job of trying to introduce some sense of order and peace. But if anything, they probably made the situation worse. In fact, Americans now suffer not only from the frontier tradition but also from the vigilante tradition which still finds its expression in the outrageous thuggery of groups such as the Ku Klux Klan.

The history of violence in America is quite unlike the history of violence elsewhere in the world. It reflects what can happen when men set out to radically reshape their modes of living and attempt to construct New Worlds from scratch. Men came to the massive continent not as tribes or communities, but as individuals fired with new ambitions and fanciful dreams. They came without social order and, from very early on, the order of nature was devalued by the fact that guns were in the hands of every man and boy. As Frantz concludes:

. . . the frontier heritage established the idea of the individual's arming himself. This activity is almost unique with the United States frontier. Instead of a central armory to which men could go to gather their arms, each man bore his own. He thus had it always at the ready. When danger arose, he would get together with another man, and another and another, until an armed mob was on its way. It might be a mob in the best posse sense, or it might be an extra-legal group which felt that its private preserves and attitudes were threatened. But it was always a mob.

The notion of a mob is quite foreign to the concept of aggro. People in a mob have only one thing in common – their immediate goal. Thus a lynch-mob, for example, is bound together solely by the task of stringing up some hapless victim on the end of a rope – there is nothing else which binds them together in any truly social sense. The mob is a collection rather than a group. The vital bonds, those which could form the basis for internal constraint based on a set of shared values, are nowhere to be found. And therefore mob violence is totally asocial. By definition it is not amenable to the processes which shape the outcomes of violence in social groups. As a result, people died in a particularly horrific way, and because the tradition of the individual, with his inalienable right to keep a gun, lives on, they continue to do so. Sadly, although Americans constantly bemoan their violence both past and present, they fail to identify what has been missing in their history. Having developed as the most powerful nation in the world without ever bothering to provide some reasonable means for coping with aggression between men in their society, they now appear rather surprised by the fact that they've got a problem at all.

The American in history carried his gun on his belt, or at least had it ready to hand above his fire-place. The 'gentleman' in Europe kept his pistols in a velvet-lined case and it took a lot of ritual to get them out. That made all the difference in terms of the patterns of violence and reflected quite fundamental differences in the management of conflict and the socialization of aggression. America failed to borrow the ceremonies of the rich European. That in itself might not be too surprising. But they also failed to adopt the ceremonies of the poor. For the noblemen of British history had by no means a monopoly on aggro.

Whilst the nobility and the upper ranks had their own special means of settling disputes, distinctive forms of aggro appeared regularly in the folk cultures of ordinary young men in Britain. In the light of modern soccer hooliganism it is interesting that the early forms of the game of football itself provided the opportunity for highly stylized rumbles: for groups of lads from neighbouring villages to engage in ceremonial battles. In the twelfth, thirteenth and fourteenth centuries the traditional Shrove Tuesday games were very energetic affairs and quite unlike the professionalized game that is now to be witnessed on Saturday afternoons. One of the earliest accounts of the folk game was given by the monk, William FitzStephen, in 1175:

All of the youth of the city go to a flat patch of ground just outside the city for the famous game of ball. The students of every faculty have their own ball, and those who are engaged in the various trades of the city also have their own ball. The older men – the fathers and the men of substance – come on horseback to watch the competitions of the younger men. In their own way the older men participate in the sporting activities of their juniors. They appear to get excited at witnessing such a vigorous exercise and by taking part in the pleasures of unrestrained youth. (*Descriptio Nobilissimae Civitatis Londinae*)

In London, these contests between the apprentices and students aroused enormous passions not only among the players but also among their associated supporters and spectators. In these cases, the game itself, which had few laid-down rules, was more of an opportunity to settle the perennial 'town-versus-gown' conflict than to engage in a detached sport.

As football became more widespread during the fourteenth and fifteenth centuries the emphasis on physical domination became progressively more pronounced. Since it was played, not by civilized lords and 'men of rank' but by common masses, violence became the subject for alarm among those in positions of power and authority. Sometimes the quarrels on the field spilled over into rather more injurious feuds after the game. But the fact that football served as a distinct social mechanism for handling aggressive rivalry is indisputable. Within the confines of the folk game, young men could establish their manly reputations without too much injury within what was essentially a convivial atmosphere. Even the Puritan, Phillip Stubbs, in his diatribe, *The Anatomy of Abuses*, concedes that this pattern of violence was rather special. He was eager to denounce it, but the essential features of aggro are still visible in his complaint:

. . . I protest unto you that it may rather be called a *frendly kinde of fyghte* than a play or recreation – a bloody and murthering practice than a felowly sport or pastime. For dooth not everyone lye in waight for his adversarie, seeking to overthrowe him and picke him on his nose, though it be uppon hard stones? In ditch or dale, in valley or hil, or what place soever it be hee careth not so he have him down. And he that can serve the most of this fashion, he is counted the only felow, and who but he?

Note that the game is seen as more of a fight, even a savage one. But it is a friendly fight. Despite Stubbs' clear denunciation of this semi-institutionalized violence, and despite action taken by the judicial courts of the day, folk football continued as a traditional way of settling old scores, local rivalries and community squabbles. Norman Elias and Eric Dunning, in their lucid account of folk football in Britain, also stress the essentially ritual nature of the so-called 'murthering practice':

> Semi-institutionalized fights between local groups arranged on certain days of the year, particularly on Saints' Days and Holy Days, were a normal part of the traditional pattern of life in medieval societies. Playing with a football was one of the ways of arranging such a fight. It was, in fact, one of the normal annual rituals of these traditional societies. To remember this institution helps us to see their manner of life in better perspective. Football and other similar encounters in those times were not simply accidental brawls. They constituted an equilibrating type of leisure activity deeply woven into the warp and woof of society. It may seem incongruous to us that, year after year, people engaged in a kind of fight on Saints' Days and Holy Days. Our forefathers, at a different stage in the civilizing process, evidently experienced it as a perfectly obvious and obviously enjoyable arrangement. ('Folk Football in Medieval and Early Modern Britain')

That violence could be 'enjoyable' is quite foreign to the dominant attitudes of modern society. But in earlier periods of our history, right up to the point where we abandoned the practice of living in recognizable communities, ritualized expressions of violent hostility were seen as contributing positively to the common good. They provided, firstly, for demonstrations of solidarity and the collective unity of a particular social group. Secondly, such rituals channelled hostility and aggression out of the group towards another, equally well-defined community of men. In fact, these two aspects of the traditional fights were intimately bound up with each other in a directly reciprocal fashion. We forget, too easily, that in-group bonds are inevitably established and reaffirmed at the expense of out-groups. And in the Shrove Tuesday football ritual there can be no better example.

By remaining at the level of a 'friendly' fight, the process operated without a lot of bloodshed. The atmosphere of a folk football game was exciting but lacking in vicious intent. These were holidays – times of festive spirit and of escape from often back-breaking labour. The violence here was fun. Fun, however, doesn't spring out of any old kind of violence. It arises when the violence is rigged in such a way that the pay-off for the participants is, on balance, in their favour. The notion of balance, though, might seem inappropriate here because some of the early 'players at football' were killed. Witness this coroner's report in the 1580s concerning the fate of Roger Ludford:

> . . . Ludford ran towards the ball with the intention to kick it, whereupon Nicholas Martyn with the forepart of his right arm and Richard Turvey with the forepart of his left arm struck Roger Ludford a blow on the forepart of the body under the breast, giving him a mortal blow and concussion of which he died within a quarter of an hour . . . .(quoted in Elias & Dunning)

To argue that violence is a balanced and socially useful ritual despite the fact that men were killed might appear to be the height of callous indifference. But what of contemporary sport? The character-enhancing virtues of 'rugger' are constantly being extolled – not least in those bastions of moral rectitude, the English public schools. In this same game, young men sometimes die. Their deaths somehow go unremarked – and yet they happen here more frequently than on the contemporary soccer terraces where 'violent demons' dwell. Ironically both 'soccer' and 'rugger' owe their existence to the Shrove Tuesday ritual fights that caused so much official alarm at the time. Because of the added formality of these games, they now meet with universal approval. But football fans, carrying on the ritual traditions of their medieval ancestors, today suffer a far heavier burden of moral and legal censure than was ever levied on the heads of folk footballers.

That aggro in the fourteenth and fifteenth centuries should have been tied to the same game which now attracts the twentieth-century 'hard men' is interesting, but, in itself, probably irrelevant. Today's ritual fighters are not players but fans. As football itself loses touch with its origins, fans appear to bring primitive notions of loyalty, solidarity and outwardly directed hostility back. But it is to the terraces, not the pitch, that these values have returned. Why soccer? Why not Rugby League for example? After all, that game bears much more of a resemblance to the tough running game of folk history.

As I suggested earlier, the venues for aggro could be accidental. Football happens to provide a useful arena on a regular basis for the aggressive activities of young men and boys. It contains other elements of masculine indulgence which might make it particularly attractive – indeed, sport-watching itself is essentially a male routine. However, these factors, I suggest, are not particularly important or persuasive. Other arenas would do just as well. The current one has lasted for ten years but is unlikely to be available for much longer. We continue to worry about football hooliganism, but its peak, most people associated with the business would agree, was back in 1973. Aggro is nomadic. It moves from place to place and from one 'host' activity to another. And the precise form of the rituals is something which is shaped by the immediate social forces of a particular point in history. The fundamental principle remains the same but each arena for masculine conflict acquires its own set of additional values and its own distinctive social definition. As the old arenas fade away young males, in search of their reputations and status, create new ones. And this they can do with surprising rapidity, as is demonstrated by the emergence of several quite separate social groups in post-war Britain for whom aggro was a prime activity. The Teddy Boys, Mods and Rockers, Skinheads and football hooligans all represented different interests and stood for different things. But these differences, which can be accounted for in terms of specific sociological theories, never quite mask the underlying strategies of aggression management which united them.

Teddy Boys are now so much a part of history that we are able to have revivals of the original Edwardian revival. The young men of the early 1950s, having now settled down to inevitable matrimonial domesticity, suddenly become cult figures. They are the men who wore drain-pipe trousers, bootlace ties and crepe-soled shoes – the very things which are now collectors' items among those too young to remember what Rock and Roll was like the first time round. The aggro men of the immediate post-war years, however, faced a hazard that was to jeopardize all of their successors – the media.

The increasing development of the media in Britain, particularly the spread of television, caused a profound change in the rise and fall of particular forms of aggressive expression. To issue high-minded proclamations, or to publish pamphlets which only a minority would read, was one thing. But to transmit moving images of neatly labelled 'outcasts' into the sitting-room of Mr and Mrs Average was another. Thousands of British folk had bought TVs to watch the Coronation in 1953. With this same machine they could now watch vivid newsreels of battles between the police and those 'sick' men in dandy costumes. And things were to get worse.

The Teddy Boys were, in many ways, rather untypical participants in the business of aggro. Principally, they had no enemies in particular – just mainstream society. Perhaps this goes some way to explaining why the movement was fairly short lived and why it eventually collapsed in violence that was anything but aggro. I include Teds in that catalogue of aggro men, however, because of the set of attitudes to which members of the movement subscribed. They belonged to distinctive groups, adopted the style of dress of an earlier age, attached themselves to the new wave of anti-establishment music, and proclaimed their willingness to fight anybody who stood in their way. Carrying a weapon was *de rigueur*, but using one was not. The Teddy Boy simply asserted his masculine right to be seen as a force to reckon with. He occupied coffee bars and reacted to harassment with aggressive defiance. He turned to the cinemas which staged Rock and Roll films and concerts, and he smashed them up when his right to dance in the aisles was challenged by the authorities. To the public and the news-hungry media of the 1950s, he presented an alarming spectacle.

Today we are quite used to disentangling some sense of reality from the web of distortion and half-truth that is weaved by journalists and media pundits. In the early post-war years, however, people still naively believed that what the papers said was true. It was there in black and white and that was that. And since sociologists had not caught on to the fact that studying working-class cultures could be academically profitable, we are left with a very distorted account of what went on. What we do know is that virtually every breach of middle-class peace in which Teddy Boys were involved made the headlines. They were easily identifiable people and little that they did escaped some form of publicity – invariably bad publicity. But when we try to examine what it was which caused so much distress to the society of the day, we find little in the way of serious injury or open savagery. Instead we find some alleged 'riots' in which groups of Teds reacted in hostile fashion when fish-and-chip shop owners refused to serve them. We find groups of young men walking through the streets of suburban towns brandishing coshes, or, more rarely, knives and bicycle chains. But 'gang murders' or 'frenzied attacks' on innocent bystanders were marked by their rarity. The only real basis for serious concern seems to have been the vandalism associated with Bill Haley concerts and films like *Rock Around the Clock*. On each occasion, the press predicted disaster, and the Teds obliged.

It's tempting to view the Teddy Boys as being similar in their activities to the theatre rowdies of the early Roman era. The Nucerians romped through the Pompeii amphitheatre, the Teds created havoc in the Odeon and the Regal. And in both cases, like

James Dean, they were rebels without a cause. They were ready for aggro but had nobody to fight. The theatre rowdies eventually found salvation at the circus. The new Edwardians of the 1950s were less fortunate. Society reacted as if violence had just been invented. Despite the fact that a world war of grotesque proportions had not long come to a catastrophic end, ordinary folk believed that men in peacock dress and greased hair were the ultimate threat to civilized existence.

It's difficult to predict what would have happened if we'd left the Teddy Boys alone and allowed them to conduct their Saturday Night at the Palais rituals without too much interference. They would probably still have broken up some tables and chairs and continued to fight among themselves. After all, Rock and Roll and Tin Pan Alley needed some excitement attached to their products in order to make them saleable. But the Teds became scapegoats for all the failings in the promise of a 'You've never had it so good' 1950s. And being very public scapegoats, they reacted publicly. They turned from being just bizarrely clad youths looking for a bit of aggro and Rock and Roll into a much less socially constrained delinquent fringe. As the clamour for retribution rose, so the violence became increasingly vicious and alienated.

When the full weight of the Law began to fall on the Teddy Boys, their numbers dwindled, and so did their cohesive unity. Any prospect of the maintenance of internal, rather than externally imposed, controls became lost as the informal social institutions which gave Teds a sense of intimate belonging and group identity were systematically broken up. Those that remained felt aggrieved and victimized, and their violence now expressed a very different ambition. They were now no longer interested just in fighting, but in shifting the burden of guilt on to some other identifiable minority group. They chose the blacks, and their swan-song was to jump onto the band wagon of racial discontent. They became involved in savage attacks on West Indians in London, and the Notting Hill Riots represented the peak of their total alienation and feelings of depersonalization. From here they faded into oblivion. Only the myths, the distortions and now, a second revival of Presley worship, remain to remind us of the satanic heydays of Rock and Roll in European History.

The story of the Teddy Boys is an illuminating one. From aggro men to race-haters – the transformation is an easy one given the presence of a system of communication that can, in presenting certain images and stereotypes, radically change the nature of people's lives. The fact that the Teds were, perhaps like contemporary soccer fans, a rather unattractive bunch, meant that even the more socially aware commentators became mixed up in the general pattern of censure and denigration. In his book *AWop-BopaLooBopLopBamBoom*, Nik Cohn does a neat hatchet job on the whole movement:

> Teds wore drain-pipe jeans, three-quarter length jackets, winkle pickers, Mississippi string ties and, mostly, they were small, skinny, spotty. They'd been nourished on rationing and tended to be underfed, rat-faced. At any rate, as teenage movements go, they were the least attractive, most malicious ever and, when roused they took out their flick knives and stabbed each other.

In the same book, however, he also points out that, 'There was nothing else to do and, right through the fifties, the Teds held command, they were the only action going. If you didn't want to join them, you had to sit indoors and vegetate.'

Despite the images which Nik Cohn has of the Teddy Boys, he recognizes that the movement met the quite explicit needs of post-war teenagers. As we've seen already, aggro always reflects, in the particular form it takes on, the social forces of a given era. In this way the timeless problems presented by aggression are easily coped with, as are the relatively more novel and socially defined problems faced by each generation of young men. But when a society begins to exploit both the needs and the scapegoat potential of such people, trouble starts. The stabbings, events which are very easy to turn into horror stories, became more frequent than we might otherwise have anticipated partly because folk expected them to occur. Even then, however, it seems that they occurred much less often than Cohn would have us believe – at least in the early days.

In deliberately trying to suppress the aggressive activities of young males in the 1950s, British society unwittingly sponsored the emergence of a far more damaging pattern of violence. The lesson of this story, though, went unrealized and the simultaneous processes of economic exploitation and amplifying media censure were brought to bear even more forcibly on the youth cultures left after the demise of the Teddy Boys. The Mods and Rockers, the exponents of aggro in the mid 1960s, became even more talked about, ridiculed and hated than any of their predecessors or historical equivalents. By now the media were able to 'package' Folk Devils so effectively, and to transmit their images to such greater numbers, that no citizens of the UK could be ignorant of their existence, nor of the alleged threat they posed to the decent way of life.

Stanley Cohen's study of the Mods and Rockers phenomenon is a sociological classic. In his book *Folk Devils and Moral Panics*, he presents most cogently a damning critique of the role which the British press played in reshaping the conduct of boys on motorbikes and scooters. His concern, as a sociologist, is with the forces which shaped the lives of these teenagers in the mid 1960s, and not with what we might see as the foundations of a pattern of activity upon which a materialist culture had put its distinctive stamp. But concerns with the 'bedrock' and with wider social and political constraints are seldom in direct conflict with each other. He saw post-war society as being subject to periods of 'moral panic'. Groups like the Teds or the Mods and Rockers appeared and became defined as threats to dominant values and interests. They were stereotyped and vilified. The conditions which give rise to such panics often just disappear. But sometimes they deteriorate and actually become more visible. And it is only by analysing the role that the media plays that this process can be understood.

The 'condition' of Mods and Rockers was one that did not submerge, or at least not immediately. Like the Teds, they simply became more visible before being beaten into obscurity by waves of quite ridiculous moral and legal retribution. Of special interest here, however, is that the phenomenon of Mods and Rockers was itself a product of the media. The Mods and Rockers evolved as quite separate and parallel youth cultures in the early sixties. Each had their distinctive tastes concerning dress and life-styles and whilst the Mods were happy to ride around on their Vespas and Lambrettas in anoraks and neatly pressed trousers, the Rockers, with their leather jackets and rather more potent BSAs, Triumphs and Nortons, were usually content to leave them alone. The real polarization into two factions came one wet weekend at Clacton in 1964 when groups of Mods and Rockers had ridden down from London for the Easter bank holiday. Local shopkeepers, perhaps irritated by the lack of trade, refused to serve a couple of 'bike boys' who were thought to be deterring customers even more than the weather. Tension between the Mods and Rockers increased and a few scuffles broke out. In the crass over-reporting of very insignificant, and only marginally violent, incidents a new arena for aggro was created overnight.

Even after the sensationalizing of the Clacton and other South Coast resort disturbances, violent conflicts between the two factions remained at a very low level. Only a few of the youths arrested were accused of 'violence against the person' – the majority being charged with offences such as breach of the peace. But the image of the Mods and Rockers was a powerful attraction to those looking for excitement and a bit of aggro. The battles on the beaches might have been more for the benefit of the television cameras than for the resolution of deep-felt animosities. But they were fights all the same. They were displays of aggression and defiance and the prospect of getting seriously injured was remote. Above all, the bike boys could engage in an expression of aggression tinged with the added excitement of illegality. In fighting the other faction, or at least going through the motions of doing so, the youth of the 1960s could also act out his antipathy to the dominant controlling interests in society and to the generation he saw as being a suppressor of his own personal values and tastes.

The violence of the Mods and Rockers never fully changed from being essentially ceremonial and constrained. Neither faction ever consisted of tightly unified social units, but the overriding, and competing, sets of values managed to endow each side with a strong identity vis-à-vis the other. Because they had a specific enemy, rather than just the intangible system against which they could rebel, the Mods and Rockers stayed in the business of ritual fighting for longer than the Teddy Boys managed to do. In the end, the Mods faded with the death of Carnaby Street – the one-time arbiter of Mod fashion and now simply a tourist rip-off. Some Rockers moved on to establish poor imitations of the Californian Hell's Angels whilst others opted for the softer option of being a Greaser. The British motorbike industry began to go broke and a moral panic subsided. But not for long. Skinheads and football hooligans were already on the road to notoriety. It was they who were truly to bring aggro back into visible existence.

Including Teddy Boys and Mods and Rockers in the historical catalogue of those involved in a distinctive pattern of conflict resolution is justified on the grounds of their marginality. That is, they are examples of youth cultures whose central aims were not to do with violence but who were still brought into the arena of violence, primarily by the press. And having got into the business of fighting, their violence never quite managed to rise to the black images which were thrust upon them. The media spoke of savage attacks, of riots and of chaotic destruction. But it never quite happened. Instead there was a lot of show, a lot of bravado – an attempt to go some way towards complying with the image, but never a total abandonment of social solutions to hostility. The non-social violence which did occur, especially towards the collapse of the Teddy Boy era, has to be understood as being caused by social and political forces external to the movement and not, in any way, as an escalation from the original fights and bundles which sparked off the train of media amplification.

In a nutshell, the rise and fall of post-war youth cultures shows us that aggro can be crushed with consummate ease by grossly and publicly distorting the reality of violent encounters. By telling people that they are doing something which they are not; by telling them that their violence is disorderly and catastrophic; by telling them that they are evil and responsible for all of society's ills, the victims of such censure start to play a new ball-game. They start to play the game we thought they were playing in the first place, but weren't.

This is not the place to try and do justice to the detailed research work which has been conducted in the last ten years or so and which has focused on the impact of both media amplification and the victims of this particularly insidious positive feedback system. The approach of the sociologists engaged in this line of inquiry is quite different from my own. But in revealing the power of communication systems in modern societies they have done much to make possible a better awareness of why aggro is now so much in danger of becoming a museum piece. My concern, in looking through the history books, has been to make a much more general statement about the long pedigree of a kind of violence which is special. I have been largely unconcerned with explanations of why aggro has emerged at various times in quite different guises, but rather with the fact that it has emerged at all. The fact that it can survive in all manner of social and political climates bears witness to its fundamental function in regulating hostile relationships among men. Equally the fact that we now seem to have reached a point in our cultural evolution where we can effect its demise is, to me, a frightening one. In America, for very special reasons, aggro never managed to get a foothold. If we want to predict what might happen in a Britain where aggro is no longer part of social life, we might do well to look at the streets of New York and Detroit – not a very promising prospect.

That, of course, is too simple. History is by no means an infallible guide to the future and America, compared with Britain and Europe, has a whole collection of other problems going for it – problems which I'm not going to ignore. But leaving less fortunate societies alone for a while, history does provide us with some material for looking in a more rational light at what often upsets us in our own society. It may not console us much that events similar to those on the contemporary soccer terraces were very familiar to the citizens of Rome and Constantinople, but at least we can look at how such events were managed in classical times. And if we compare their guarded tolerance with our own abysmal panic we might learn something very important. We should learn that aggro poses only an illusory threat when compared with the very different violence which can be inculcated in the wake of reality-changing, outraged censure. 'Better the Devil you know' might well be an apposite sentiment here. But first you have to know your Devil.

The contrast between aggro and other types of violence, whether such contrasts are made at a sociological, ethological, anthropological or historical level, means that attention has to be given to the other side of the violent coin. I've tried to spell out what aggro is made of and how it works, but to assess its value and importance we are forced to look at patterns of conflict which are made of something else. We are also forced to pay more attention to one feature of conflicts that, so far, I have only touched upon – territories. Much of aggro has been closely associated with defence of a territory of one sort or another, whether it be an End on a football terrace or a club house near the Roman hippodrome. Equally territories of a very different kind have been the ostensible basis for some of the deadliest wars in the history of mankind. In moving towards some evaluation of aggro, in contrast with other less savoury trials of strength, the importance of sorting out the nature of territoriality becomes very important – especially since the concept has become much abused in recent years.

5

The Territorial Confusion

The notion of territoriality is one which has figured prominently in many popular explanations of why men fight each other. Men fight, it is suggested, because they are trying to defend marked-out boundaries of one kind or another, and sometimes this is indeed the case. But it is by no means always the case. Even more importantly, the sorts of boundaries that are fought over can vary a great deal. There remains, however, a strong suspicion in the minds of many people that aggression and territoriality are very much part of the same process and have, fundamentally, the same origins in nature. Along with this suspicion is held the assumption that territoriality in man is directly comparable with territoriality in animals – both being instinctive and immutable.

Robert Ardrey in his book *The Territorial Imperative* stands out as one of the main advocates of this line of thought.

> A territory is an area of space, whether of water, or earth or air, which an animal or group of animals defends as an exclusive preserve. The word is also used to describe the inward compulsion in animal beings to possess and defend such a space. A territorial species of animals, therefore, is one in which all males, and sometimes females too, bear an *inherent drive* to gain and defend an exclusive property.
> ... Man ... is as much a territorial animal as the mocking bird singing in the clear Californian night. We act as we do for reasons of our evolutionary past, not our cultural present, and our behaviour is as much a mark of our species as is the shape of a human thigh bone ....

The trouble with Ardrey's picture of man's instinctive territoriality is that it seems so immediately plausible and convenient. Accepting, uncritically, his assumptions promises to solve some of the all-too-common features of our present way of life. After all, don't we have nations with rigid frontiers, and are we not prepared to die

95

in the name of our country, our territorial identity? 'My country, right or wrong.' And surely, we live in our own immediate territories – our houses with their gardens and their wooden fences. 'Trespassers keep out.' We seek to isolate our immediate family group. 'The Englishmen's home is his castle.' We defend it from would-be violators. We need special documents and passports to cross frontiers which might often amount to nothing more than imaginary lines which separate two identical and unremarkable strips of earth. On a similar but smaller scale, our village, town, city or country becomes something which adds to our personal identity. The Yorkshire man, born and bred, is proud of that fact. Being a native of Barnsley sets you apart from men who live elsewhere; and with other men from Barnsley, no matter in what unlikely place you chance to meet them, you have an immediate affinity.

We seem to be surrounded by territories of one sort or another everywhere. At first glance it may seem that our territoriality and our aggression are inextricably bound up with each other. Wars are between nations and fights are often to do with those rivals from another town, another housing estate or another street. It all seems so obvious. And this is why the ideas of men like Ardrey catch on so quickly and· receive such widespread and uncritical acceptance. Territoriality becomes the key to understanding man's 'instinctive' violence – his urge to kill in order to protect his patch, his little acre.

There may, of course, be something in all this. On the other hand there are two critical tests we must apply to such a thesis. Firstly, to what extent are other animals territorial – is this territorial instinct that Ardrey believes in so passionately a widespread feature of nature? Secondly, to what extent are the territories of man comparable with the territories of other animals? Two very simple questions but, surprisingly, ones which seem all too often to be completely avoided.

In the cursory examination of aggression in other animals it was quite clear that conflicts often arose when a conspecific male entered the marked-out area of another. In the case of the stickleback or the Siamese fighting fish it's clear that these species don't simply swim around haphazardly in the pond which supports them. Instead they endlessly patrol only a very small portion of it. The particular boundaries they create may not be very visible – there are relatively few potential sources of demarcation in the water – but the trespassing of another male is often an immediate cause of hostile displays and fighting. Other fish, however, differ very widely in the extent to which they show any territoriality at all. Great variations also exist within a single species. It has been reported that fish such as cichlids and bass defend certain marked-out areas in circumstances where the availability of food resources is limited. But in abundant flowing waters they display no territorial behaviour at all. Among primates the picture is a similarly confusing one. Chimps and gorillas are largely free-ranging animals and show few signs of defending marked-out boundaries. On the other hand, troops of baboons, in some habitats, are extremely territorial and will defend their areas very fiercely against other groups of conspecifics. It is the baboon which is Robert Ardrey's particular favourite – the 'outrageous' success of evolution and all based, he claims, on the animal's dominant, territorial behaviour. Even the baboon, however, is capable of successful living without such ostentatious defence of his frontiers. As Ashley Montagu points out in *The Nature of Human Aggression*, there is a good deal of ethological evidence to suggest that separate groups of baboons, even in highly populated areas, come into contact with each other almost daily and show not the slightest aggression as a result. He also goes on to provide a list of other species who have never been observed to engage in anything resembling territorial behaviour. Among such species he includes animals as diverse as field mice, zebras, mountain goats, deer, rhesus monkeys and wallabies. There is no basis for believing that males of these species never enter into aggressive conflicts with each other. But these conflicts rarely have anything to do with the defence or violation of territory.

Ardrey's claim for a basic instinct, one which is somehow bound up with that of aggression, starts to wear a little thin. Put simply, there is evidence that indicates a strong pattern of territorial behaviour in some, but certainly not all, species of animals. This behaviour, however, very often appears to be related to a specific adaptation to the surrounding habitat rather than to some general instinctive or 'wired-in' process. The fact that some animals are territorial in one environment and not in another does a great deal of damage to the notion of there being a simple genetic factor· operating.

Whether or not animals engage in territorial behaviour seems to be very much related to the ecological conditions in which they find themselves. Those living in plentiful surroundings have little need to carve up the habitat into defended feeding or hunting areas, and by and large they don't. Where basic resources are less abundant, territoriality is a logical response. It ensures the dispersion of the population in relation to the availability of food. In many species it not only disperses but effectively limits the birth-rate. In some cases the opportunities to mate only come when a territory has been

The Territorial Confusion

satisfactorily established. The African wildebeest, for example, stands no chance of wooing a receptive female unless he has first of all managed to stake out his own little piece of the savanna. To be an eligible bachelor he must demonstrate his material wherewithal to sustain and raise a family. Territoriality is one of many potential adaptations to fluctuating ecological circumstances. At best, therefore, we can only accept that there is a broad inherited striving for regulation which requires subsequent experience to give direction. Territories are one source of regulation, and they can be very effective. But their existence doesn't, logically, imply an 'instinct package' containing both the marking out and aggressive defence drives. Aggressive behaviour is sometimes a consequence of the existence of territories. But the existence of an aggressive process doesn't, in any necessary way, lead to the creation of territories. That is a quite separate matter. Aggression only comes into play when territories need to be defended. In many cases that might not be very often.

What I am really saying is there are overpowering reasons to believe that aggression is rooted in nature – that animals have aggression because, like sex, it is an essential aspect of their biological make-up. Aggression is a prerequisite for continual survival and for the manipulation of the material and social world. But this has nothing to do with territoriality in a direct sense, and to parcel the two together into one global genetic package is a mistake. Animals vary in the extent to which they fight each other. They also vary in their levels of reproductivity. Aggression is clearly present in species which are normally quite amicable and docile, and despite the fact that some animals are more sexy and promiscuous than others, all species still get reproduced. Territoriality, however, comes and goes. Some animals have it and some don't. Some species have it some of the time and are quite happy without it on other occasions. Animals can be aggressive without territories and when territories exist they don't always lead to aggressive defending behaviour – it depends on what an animal takes to be a violation of its territory.

Where territories exist and where these territories require defending, a new impetus is given to the struggle for the ritualization of aggression. A new source of potential conflict comes into existence. Within a group of animals, males need to settle problems of dominance and status – they have to manage the 'pecking-order' in a way that doesn't cause too much damage. Where border disputes are concerned, whether they be between groups or between individuals, similar solutions are required. In some species there

98

appear to be more conflicts concerning dominance than territoriality. In others, the reverse is the case.

In man it often appears that aggro includes both the striving for dominance and the territorial aspects. I have tried to suggest already that we don't need to buy a simple-minded aggressive instinct theory – at least not in the chilling form that it usually appears. What I want to do now is to suggest that there are no direct parallels between territoriality in animals, where it exists, and the territories of man, especially those which are most closely associated with ritual aggro. Aggro often centres around territories of a kind, but we can now begin to stand that 'territorial imperative' on its head. The 'defensible turf' kind of territory which often features strongly in aggressive rituals, is not based on a need to gain access to any vital resource. It is simply an area which is given limited access to particular rival groups by its defenders.

The apparent need, particularly among young men and boys in Western society, for home 'turf' results in highly distinctive and recognizable social phenomena. Football fans stake out their pieces of terracing and create Ends. As we have seen, violation of this 'sacred' space is frequently the immediate cause of the severest conflict displays. In America, the territorially based rivalries between opposing groups have been even more fully documented. Louis Yablonsky's book *The Violent Gang* is a classic account of how in Chicago, years after the decline of Al Capone and the Syndicate mobsters, young working-class kids carved up the city into a whole matrix of zones. Each zone 'belonged' to a closely knit, and often seriously delinquent, gang which firmly resisted any advances from would-be violators.

There are, however, some very important differences between this characteristically human defence of turf and the territorial behaviour of other animal species. There is no question of excluding everyone else except your own immediate group. In fact a 'gang' is always composed of only a very small proportion of the people who live within its territorial confines. Similarly the End of the football ground is defended only against other young fans of opposing teams who are kitted out in the same way, and who share, fundamentally, the same set of values. In Chicago, Glasgow or any other city which is host to rival street gangs, people cross and re-cross the nominal boundaries without even being aware of them. In South London they may notice lines such as 'Catford Boot Boys Rule OK', daubed with aerosol paint on the walls. But they are hardly likely to interpret this as indicating that they have no business walking into this particular area.

These territories have a very special function. I suggest that they are created in order to enable the social control of male aggression. This is in direct contrast with other animal territories which, as a by-product, serve to arouse aggression. Human territories of the defensible turf kind are, as one American sociologist nicely puts it, behaviour facilitating. In other words the social activities of many people, young men in particular, would have no meaning unless distinctive arenas existed in which they could take place. The soccer End is what endows football aggro with sense. It provides the young vociferous inhabitants with a collective identity – a 'tribal' identity without which the ceremonial battles would have no meaning at all. Because territories are behaviour facilitating, rather than behaviour restricting, which is the case among other animals, they positively encourage the contemporary forms of social management of male conflicts. The conflicts, stemming from aggression which has nothing to do with territoriality in a direct sense, can be focused around new and socially defined territories. Arenas and discrete 'stages' emerge. As a result, conflicts are contained and the means of safely dealing with aggression are given a healthy boost. The 'turf' areas don't cause aggression, although it might look that way sometimes. Their true function is to allow men and boys to act out their aggression in a safe and orderly way.

Without marked-out and well-defined arenas, aggro would lack much of its directing force. Conflicts could still be ritualized but some other basic social framework would have to come into play. There would have to be some other mechanism which both served to unite a group and provided a special context in which stylized fighting could take place.

The whole argument might sound a little tenuous and far-fetched. Wouldn't it be simpler to refer to the territorial instinct, one which impels people to mark out patches and which subsequently leads to imperialistic quarrels? Well, yes it might. But simple answers to perennial questions are not always the right ones. To make the statement that men need certain kinds of territories in order to have effective arenas for the management of their aggression is, perhaps, to turn some very widespread theories upside down. But I am not suggesting that all aspects of territorial behaviour in man have this function. I am talking about the notion of a home turf – an area, usually urban, that is held by only a distinct minority of the people who live within it and defend it only against an equally distinct minority who live outside of it. It's as if one man says to another: 'Look, here is a line I have drawn in the sand. Step over it and I will attack you, keep away from it and you are chicken.' It's as basic as that. The imaginary boundaries of Chicago or the very real steel ones at soccer grounds come to have significance only when groups of rivals agree that they are like the lines in the sand – when they accept the implied challenge which they present to their dominance and masculine power. When the otherwise unremarkable street-corner divisions or the cold metal terrace railings take on this extra symbolic aspect, then putting down one's rival is capable of becoming an equally symbolic affair – a ritual in the true sense of the word.

The existence of these special techniques is no guarantee that conflicts will be ritualized. Street gangs in Chicago often did each other considerable damage and *West Side Story* is probably over-romantic in this respect. But the business could have been considerably more bloody than it was. To some extent, America came closer to having opportunities for aggro here. They never fully materialized and the racial conflicts which subsequently over-shadowed the more everyday aggressive encounters in city streets probably put paid to it altogether. But where such problems are less endemic, the existence of symbolic demarcations can facilitate, in a very positive way, the management of aggression.

The whole aggro business often involves a kind of territoriality but not the kind which sparks off fierce attacks in other animals. The animal needs his territory because without it he can't eat and he can't mate either. The soccer fan needs his territory only in the sense that without it he and his mates would have to go off and find some other means of fighting with other kids in a way that didn't involve too many broken bones or bleeding bodies.

From this it's quite clear that a simplistic and global concept of the territorial imperative is just not going to work. If we try to interpret events on the soccer terraces, or even in the streets of present-day Glasgow, in the light of such assumed instincts we would get the explanation totally wrong. We would assume that males were fighting because of something in their nature which drove them to create and defend their little empires. As we have seen, it works the other way round. Men have these kinds of territories because they want to fight. Getting rid of simple-minded notions, however, doesn't mean that we have to abandon a concept of territoriality altogether. It may very well be that the appearance of a whole spectrum of marked-off spaces in a majority of human communities is indicative of very basic needs that man, for one reason or another, has acquired. These needs may still not arise out of instinct and the territories have little in common with those to be found elsewhere in the natural world. By considering the changes which took place in man's evolution from a nomadic hunting tribesman to a settled farmer and town-dweller, we might come up with a rather different explanation for this apparent desire to surround ourselves with boundaries.

A species which consists mainly of small hunter-gatherer communities is one which is essentially nomadic. Tribes may colonize and, at times, defend, particular hunting and supportive areas. But usually these areas are only temporary. They, like the territories of animals, are solutions to problems raised by changes in population and variations in the ecological surroundings. The space is used, the tribe moves on, and new sections of the habitat are developed. At this level, man's territoriality has quite a lot in common with that of other mammalian, predominantly hunting, species. It is about preservation and allocation of essential resources – the border defences are to do with the struggle for survival. In the case of the Maring, this preservation of the clearings doesn't, at first sight, appear to be very adaptive, but territorial behaviour is still directly instrumental in maintaining a realistic balance between a community and its material world.

Western man, however, has moved away from the dominant patterns of hunting and gathering and of cutting and burning. He rarely hunts because the animals he needs for food are now tamed and kept in docile captivity. Similarly his plantations have become permanent. He no longer needs to cut and then to move on in order that the vegetation can regenerate. Efficient farming techniques, which emerged long before the recent introduction of modern nurseries and glasshouses, meant that food became a predictable and static commodity. It is true that droughts and floods could reduce entire populations to the level of starvation, but the set-backs became less and less frequent than those experienced by our nomadic ancestors.

Once the basic resources for existence became fixed in particular places, it was the permanent boundary which now surrounded man's territories. Dry stone wall enclosures stopped cattle straying out of easy reach – that was their true function. But they also came to symbolically announce the lasting ownership of the space. Whilst hedges and ditches kept the animals in, they became ultimately a means of keeping other men out.

With the establishment of static communities came, perhaps for the first time, the real possibilities for advance in technology and in commercial trading. Developments in the Iron Age, for example, demanded the kinds of facilities which simply could not be carried around. And although trading was often conducted by wandering entrepreneurs, they still relied on the goods produced by the farmers and artisans of permanent villages and encampments. This kind of transition, in itself, might go a long way to explain the current obsession which people exhibit for their own enclosures. We might well accept that the transition was originally achieved with the help of some adaptive drive rooted in man's nature. The will of the community to mark out and protect, a legacy inherited by early hunting *Homo*, might justifiably be seen as a facilitating factor in our species' evolution towards a sedentary existence – towards a pattern of living which has made civilization possible. The transition having been made, the legacy lapses. 'Latent territoriality', if such an idea has any true meaning at all, has as much to do with the emergent cultural frameworks as it has with anything still lurking in the human genetic catalogue. Once the habit of creating boundaries that are permanent, or at least intended to be permanent, is established, virtually all of the aspects of territoriality we now take for granted follow. They are there not because we, like dogs, have some apparent need to cock our legs and leave our scent on the areas around our own backyards. They are there because we have made a strategic move away from the restrictions which nature once put upon us. In the process we have created a pattern of living which has a passing resemblance to some aspects of the life-styles of some other animals. But the simple equation is broken. That is why our territories look different, have different effects, and have such enormous variations.

We have already seen that the home turfs which are associated with some contemporary manifestations of aggro require a radical overhaul of the standard territorial imperative notion. Having made this overhaul, however, we can afford to be a little less dogmatic. I still want to make use of the notion of territoriality. But I don't want to buy all the trimmings of Ardrey's approach at the same time. Not only are they not needed, they get in the way.

Nevertheless this does not preclude us from making use of the findings of ethology. It just means that we have to be a damned sight more careful when we apply them to man. And equally, we have to remember the very basic transitions which now put us at one remove from even the smartest of other primates.

Once we accept that, the notion of territoriality can provide us with a key to understanding other patterns of violence within our society. It can also help us to see more clearly why aggro is very different from other expressions of aggression. Aggro doesn't actually require any element of territoriality at all. But where special kinds of territory can be established the ritualization of aggression in man can be made more easy to achieve. Other forms of violence, on the other hand, stem directly from territoriality. But here the territories are of a very different nature. Some kinds of violence even result from the absence of certain kinds of territory. Thus, in order to see aggro for what it really is, and to put its relationship with territoriality in proper context, we are obliged to consider these other patterns of violence more carefully. To understand why ritual resolutions of conflict are so important to man's survival as a civilized species we need to look at the roots not only of aggro but of the infinitely more damaging violence that is characterized not by ceremony but by bloodshed.

One aspect of our own territorial way of life owes something to nature in a very special way. It stems from the fact that we are a pair-bonding species and we give birth to offspring who are totally dependent on adults for a very considerable length of time. All human societies have centred around the distinctive breeding unit – the male and the female living together in a distinctively bonded way. Given the fact that babies and children need mothers and, arguably, fathers for upwards of seven years, pair-bonding is a pretty basic requirement for survival. We can put up with a certain level of adultery, divorce, polygamy and so on. But the family and the responsibilities of stable parenthood have been the core of societies throughout history and throughout the world. One of the consequences of this by-and-large monogamous way of life is the marital home. Like birds we build nests and like birds we defend our nests. But unlike birds our nests become centres for a very complex flow of social behaviour. The robin doesn't invite neighbouring robins in for drinks and a chat. He attacks any bird who comes near. We don't. That's why our 'defensible spaces' need looking at very closely.

One robin's nest is much like another. There are few sources of individual variations. The man and his family, however, whether it be extended or nuclear, is the literal home territory which becomes an ideal resource for the achievement of identities. The expression 'a house is not a home' tells us a lot. It means that the basic territorial space, established by the erection of four walls, a roof and, perhaps, a small piece of land, is not enough. To be worth defending it has to have an essential symbolic character stamped upon it. Without this stamp, this personal identification, the area becomes a source of alienation rather than of social affiliation.

Personalization takes many forms and in modern society, where identities are less easy to come by than in the traditional tribal community, it becomes a major requirement for truly social existence. We like our box to be different from the boxes next to it. We like to give our houses names even though the postman might require only a number. In particular, we make use of the internal spaces in extremely idiosyncratic ways. The house becomes an extension of the family – a visible summary of its attitudes, ambitions and personal tastes. When we defend our home we defend something which is us. We defend it like we defend our own body. In the same way that we regularly invite entry to our bodies or to the area that immediately surrounds them, we can also use our homes to welcome intimacy.

Defence of home space arises only when entry to them is seen to be illegitimate. When this essentially private space is violated we resist, and our resistance can take the form of the most violent measures available to us. The thief in the night is not a man with whom we enter into a ritual conflict resolution procedure. We take a heavy object and we smash it over his head. And such behaviour is unlikely to be the subject of censure. The attitude that a man may take almost limitless steps to defend his home is even embodied in the legal system of virtually all developed societies. Actually killing an intruder may sometimes be thought to be going a little too far, but even here, a charge of murder is unlikely to follow. It is more likely to be manslaughter or justifiable homicide.

The point here is that the violence associated with home defence is quite unlike the violence which is associated with symbolic boundaries of street gangs and football terraces. The aggro which centres around the equivalents of lines in the sand has much in common with the ritualized territorial conflicts in some other animal species. But the territories themselves have little in common. The territory of the home looks more like those created by other pair-bonding animals, only in this case the violence is of a very different kind. There is rarely even the possibility of ritualizing our defensive aggression here because we refuse, in the main, to enter into a social relationship with violators, and we don't try to run up a special framework in which to manage the immediate conflict.

That violation of one's home is very much like violation of one's body is borne out by the testimony of people who have been burgled. They say that their home feels 'unclean' afterwards. The fact that someone has entered it and defiled it is so often of more consequence than the objects or money that have been stolen. Some unknown and uninvited person has delved into somebody else's extension of themselves – an extension which can only be displayed or given access to those with whom one shares some elementary social relationship. The burglar becomes like the rapist who invades the ultimate privacy. Everything he touches becomes symbolically soiled.

The Territorial Confusion

The body and its extension, the home, constitute the most basic of intimate territories and the violence which arises when they need defending reflects their special nature. On the other hand, the inability to create these extensions can also lead to patterns of violence which are quite unlike the ceremonial affairs with which we have been concerned. What happens when the opportunities for personal identification are made unavailable because of the physical structure of living units? What follows when houses can no longer be so easily converted into homes?

An American architect, Oscar Newman, has paid particular attention to the effects that various housing policies have had on the lives of families and their children. In particular, he has been concerned with the violence and crime which is often associated with one particular form of housing development – the high-rise apartment block. If anyone doubts that such an association exists he should give serious attention to what goes on both within and around the towers of concrete that have sprung up around major town and cities in both the United States and in Britain.

For some time people assumed that the effects of tower blocks could be accounted for simply in terms of overcrowding. Studies with animals show quite conclusively that if you pack them into confined spaces and exceed a certain density they get cross. The same thing happens with people, although here the picture is predictably more complicated. In our everyday lives we quite happily tolerate very extreme forms of overcrowding. Travelling on tube trains in the rush hour we stand in full body contact with total strangers. We temporarily suspend the claim to a territorial zone around ourselves and seem none the worse for wear. On the football terraces we actually welcome this sustained physical closeness. Without it the whole atmosphere and excitement of the game is reduced – it doesn't seem right.

Even in our homes we often cope well with permanently high densities and, in relative terms with distinct overcrowding. In fact, it is only since the eleventh century, when the efficient chimney flue first made its appearance, that we in Britain could begin efficiently to divide our living spaces into separate and private isolated areas. Before then the entire family sat huddled for warmth around open fires placed in the middle of a hall-like area, often with unglazed windows. One couldn't sneak off to the den or to the bedroom because it would have been too cold, in winter at least. The space might have been available but it couldn't be used.

When we look at high-rise blocks we find that although the density is high it is often no higher than some low-rise housing estates where the levels of violence and crime are much lower. So what is the real distinguishing feature? Oscar Newman points out that homes, no matter where in the world one chooses to look, have traditionally had some interesting features to them. One aspect which appears to be very significant is the way in which the entrance is constructed. He draws our attention to 'stoops' which are the characteristic porches to be found outside houses from Pompeii to Papua. They serve as a kind of transition and provide an intermediate area between the private inner space of the home and the public space in the street. The disinctive entrance assists demarcation of territory because visitors can be 'held' in this in-between social space until their credentials have been checked. Newman suggests that when this entry space is neglected in the design of things, problems arise. And they arise because people no longer feel that they have defensible space. The limit comes, he suggests, when more than four living units share a single entrance – in particular when the entrance to apartments is not visible to the occupants. A high-rise block may have hundreds of apartments, access to which is initially given via a single entrance on the ground floor. On the living floors the doors to the apartments themselves open directly onto long corridors – there is no stoop or porch to provide a transition from home to public space.

Under these conditions, territories cease to be easily identified. Strangers can come and go unchallenged through the main entry point. The corridors cannot be subject to surveillance from inside the apartments because no windows open onto them. The territory of the home can only be defended by locking doors and fitting chains. Individual family units shrink further away from an involvement in the community around them. Vandalism goes unchecked. Violence erupts not in defence of territory, but because the territories are 'non-defensible' except in the wholly negative sense. The opportunities for personalizing identities have gone. Without the security of spaces that are extensions of character itself, surrounded by symbolic boundaries which interrupt the flow of movement from public to inner zones, the ways in which people behave towards one another change radically. Violence, when it is witnessed in or around tower blocks, goes unchallenged because there are no symbolic boundaries to define it as being within one's sphere of interference or social control. The network of social relationships, essential to the proper management of aggression, is no longer available. The tower block fails to recreate a tribe or a community. It creates instead a collection of individual families unconcerned with the activities of each other and equally unconcerned with what happens immediately outside their door. Their territory exists only when the door is shut.

As a striking illustration of the direct effect that architecture can have on the management of violence, Oscar Newman and his colleagues made a tape-recording of a simulated marital quarrel. The tape-recorder was taken into a high-rise block of apartments and the playback volume turned up. As the quarrel proceeded, nobody came near to find out what was happening. As the quarrel became more violent, those within earshot began to lock their doors. The sound of chains being fixed could be heard along the corridor. Nobody wanted to know. The violent episode went on unchecked and unmanaged by the surrounding community.

For a comparison, the researchers set out to play the recording in a low-rise 'walk-up' housing system – a block where each small group of apartments had its own disinctive entrance. The problem here was that of getting the tape-recorder through the entry without being seen. A group of strangers with bulky equipment, passing through a clearly symbolized intermediate zone, was subjected to immediate attention and interest by the residents. When the recording was played back, the response was even more immediate. People in the other apartments wanted to know what was happening. Instead of locking themselves in they felt a need to intervene in the violence they assumed was being perpetrated in their community. The space outside their doors was not just public, and therefore of no concern to them. It was communal, and very much within their orbit of interest and influence.

Governments and local authorities are only just beginning to realize the importance that people attach to the very special territories with which they seek to surround themselves. The notorious Pruit Igo high-rise apartment blocks in the USA have been literally blown up because of the catastrophic effect they produced on people's social lives. In Britain we have probably witnessed an end to the rapid construction of tower blocks such as those which stand like concrete monuments to unthinking and irresponsible planners on the outskirts of Birmingham and other major cities. Though we must all wonder whether the true lesson of territoriality has been properly learnt.

We thus have an odd state of affairs. The territories which man creates can be seen both as precipitators of aggression and as instruments of aggression management. Violence may erupt when boundaries are disputed, but violence can become largely symbolic and non-injurious when boundaries serve to define arenas in which conflict can be socially contained. In addition, the lack of certain territories can result in an increase in violence because the social control of conflict relies heavily on the ability of people to see conflicts as being within their sphere of influence. To be involved in the social management process people need not only a secure and personalized territory that is their home, but also an extension of their home into communally owned, rather than faceless and alienating space. Man, in contrast to the mocking bird, begins to appear a most peculiar territorial animal.

Fundamentally the relationship between territories and the patterns of violence among men is significant but indirect. Territories, however they come to be constructed, and whatever their nature, are the things from which conflicts and rivalries can arise. But the manner in which these conflicts are solved has to do with the social frameworks which exist in relationship to those territories, not with the notion of territoriality itself. Some territories, those which are created within the context of distinctive social frameworks, lead to conflicts which are easily managed. In the process, wider conflicts to do with dominance and status can also be resolved. This happens when it is the striving for social dominance itself, and for the putting down of rivals, which is responsible for the creation of those territories in the first place. In contrast, the existence of some territories becomes established for reasons quite unrelated to aggression – a major factor being to do with our pair-bonding habits. We create homes and these homes become, next to the body itself, the prime defensible spaces. This again is not too problematic because our homes, like our bodies, are only rarely violated. The existence of elaborate legal codes to do with trespass, illegal entry, criminal damage, burglary and so on gives us some means of coping with actual or attempted violations. As a last resort, we bring into play our capacity to use weapons with violent and bloody consequences. But this level of violence poses little threat to our species as a whole. We may be territorial animals in this sense but few of us have strong desires to annex the home of our next-door neighbour.

The third kind of territoriality, however, does present us with a problem. This is a large-scale version which arises out of the fact that we have made the transition from nomadic hunter-gatherer tribal communities to static agriculturalists. Because of their fixed locations, our communities have progressively become larger. Bigger and more distinctive boundaries have developed to surround the closed collections of farms, the raw materials of developing technologies and the people who rely upon them. Through the encampments of early man, the village communities, the city state, the princedom, the kingdom, new alliances, new communications –

we end up with nations and even collections of nations. The Western world, the Eastern world, the Third world – the new megaliths – the power blocks emerge as the ultimate territories. All this is a long way from the line in the sand. It is also a long way from the territory of the home and the collections of homes. Man has indeed built upon nature but in the process he has constructed national equivalents of the high-rise block.

The territories of nations have no equivalent in the animal world. Nations are not natural units, nor are they social units. We may feel proud of the fact that we are British or French or American. The fact that we live in a particular country may give us an identity of a kind, depending on the extent of our chauvinism. But what does it mean to say that we belong to a group of 50 million or 300 million or a 1,000 million when our social relationships rarely involve more than 100 or so people? In *The Naked Ape* Desmond Morris shows that our social networks reach out only about as far as the traditional size of a tribe. In the midst of essentially unnatural urban environments we still seem to cling to something rooted deep in our history and in our nature. We don't want, nor can we achieve, a social bond with an entire national population.

All of this has dire implications for the violence which erupts as a result of the existence of national boundaries. Putting down a rival who competes with us in the informal or formal hierarchy stakes is a social event, or at least it is capable of being so. That is what aggression is really all about. Going to war is not a social event, nor is it capable of ever being so. War is about a roomful of men in one country directing action against a roomful of men in another country, and no amount of 'hot-lines' will turn that into a social encounter. In between these two rooms men die. They die not because the thing has gone wrong but because it is the simple intention of the men in the two rooms that they should do so. A battlefield is not the place to engage in ceremony or ritual. It is the place to kill or be killed, or both. And this whole tragic business comes about not because of man's nature but because man has moved too far away from his nature. There is no reason whatsoever to suppose that the wholesale killing of men by men has anything to do with his biological inheritance. Man alone is the slayer of his own species. He has achieved this distinction because he, and only he, has been able to put a gulf between himself and his biological roots. An ironical product of all this is the ability to become a kind of hunter again. But now the prey is other men.

6

The Hunting Factor

A look at a few of the complexities inherent in the concept of territoriality has allowed for a more meaningful separation of aggro from the other patterns of violence with which it is too often confused. We have some idea of the roots, both natural and cultural, upon which aggro rests, and of the new territories which have come to be associated with injury and death. But the existence of territories cannot fully explain why men are able to kill. To understand why some conflicts are ritualized whilst others are not we need to examine how man, in distancing himself from nature, has made possible a revival of certain features of his primal heritage – his ability to hunt.

There are a number of good reasons to suppose that hunting behaviour and fighting stem from different sources. The most obvious and compelling of these is that the behaviours themselves take on distinctly different forms. In hunting the aim is simply to kill for food. There is no ceremony or ritual in the proper sense here. Instead the most effective means are employed to achieve the end required. Fighting with a rival is often the least effective (in the sense of physically damaging) course that is pursued. Whilst fighting may involve adrenalin and excitement, killing an animal can be conducted in cold-blooded calm and detachment. It is true that the chase may bring out anticipation and elation, but these aren't essential. It is the group which stealthily tracks and silently surrounds its prey, rather than the mob who run screaming and shouting, which is likely to be the best fed.

Hunting leads to killing. Subduing a rival leads, under normal circumstances, to a ritual. To make a bit of a leap, if we want to understand why men kill each other, why they commit acts of almost unimaginable atrocity against their fellows, we should look not to aggression, as we have used the concept so far, but towards what has been called, presumptuously, the 'hunting instinct.'

Early man, as he evolved from the fruit-picking nomadic primate, developed an appetite for meat and a primitive drive to hunt because that, presumably, was in his best interests at the time. If such behaviour was other than a necessary adaptation to prevailing ecological conditions, *Homo sapiens* would have had a rather shorter history than the one he has enjoyed. In many areas of the world, communities still exist where hunting prey is a requirement for survival. The rest of us, on the other hand, have made a more sensible arrangement. Instead of having to expend a lot of energy running after our food, we pen it up on farms. We breed out those characteristics of our prey we find undesirable until we have a nice, docile, manageable and domesticated herd or flock that can be turned into protein by a quick trip to the local abattoir. And yet we still seem to want to go on hunting. Ironically it is now the indulgence of the rich on their grouse moors and deer parks to continue this ancient pattern of activity. Our hunting past, however, lives on in many other taken-for-granted features of the societies we live in. Many sports for example are to do with sharp objects projected at a target or hurled over a great distance. The act of pursuit itself seems to have no reason to it unless we remember that fleetness of foot was often a requirement for obtaining a supper.

The fact that hunting behaviour remains, even in societies which have absolutely no call for it, may seem mysterious. Again there has been an immediate rush to seize upon the notion of instinct and catch-all kinds of explanation. In the case of aggression, however, we have seen that instinct theories are not necessary. Whilst we migh allow as plausible the inheritance of a rather broad but weak drive to dominate and subdue, we needn't buy the aggressive gene notion completely. We don't need to because it is possible that cultures can carry on, at a very basic level, doing the work that nature once did for herself. But what about hunting behaviour?

Hunting behaviour can be divided into two aspects. The first has to do with chasing, stalking, having speed and a good aim. The second has to do with a determination and will to kill. Early tribes needed both of these factors to survive. Their cultures, therefore, took great pains to ensure that the complete hunting package figured strongly in the basic teachings of mythology and folklore. Hunters had special status; young boys aspired to such roles and even their play was geared towards such an end. As societies progressed towards domestication only one aspect of hunting behaviour was now required – the killing part. You couldn't simply wait for one of your pigs to grow old and die, possibly from some disease which would render it inedible. You had to go and cut its throat. So killing remained. The chasing and aiming were no longer needed for survival. But instead of simply discarding them they were retained because of their social spin-offs. Sport and games have great utility in any culture. They provide for leisure, the establishment of new kinds of bonds and for physical fitness itself. Add to such activities the competitiveness associated with aggression and you have a major and recognizable aspect of virtually all modern communities.

Again it is possible that some broad instinctive basis for hunting behaviour still remains floating around in the human gene pool. But culture can keep such things alive just as easily. In both the case of aggression and of hunting, whether we stress the biological or cultural aspects will probably have more to do with our own private philosophies of mankind itself than with the rational weighing of evidence. Evidence, in a form that is testable, is notoriously difficult to come by in the nature/culture debate. But if nothing else, we should at least question the simplistic assumptions made by extremists on both sides. Robert Ardrey, in a couple of very popular best-selling books *African Genesis* and *The Territorial Imperative*, argued at great length, and not without a lucid prose style, that man's primeval hunting activities were the result of an emerging slayer species; a species with a bloodlust picking up weapons and killing his fellows with the same relish that he killed his food. It is the picture of the archetypal savage, the cannibalistic murdering member of a super species who makes progress only through butchery. The threads of Ardrey's argument are drawn together in a more recent book which summarizes his view of man and which is appropriately entitled *The Hunting Hypothesis*. On the frontispiece of this book is a quote:

> While we are members of the intelligent primate family, we are uniquely human even in the noblest sense, because for untold millions of years we alone killed for a living.

Little wonder, many conclude from the gloomy prophecies within the covers of this book, that our history is littered with corpses of the million upon million who stood in the way of primitive greed and violent ambitions. One fundamental aspect of hunting behaviour – one which stares us in the face – is obscured by this foul image. It is the fact that all hunting is predicated on the killing of things that are not us. The deer is not a man. The deer is edible. We kill the deer. The assumption made by people like Ardrey is that killing the deer, or the bison, or the bird leads us inevitably to kill each other. But he forgets to mention that in order to kill another man we must first of all accomplish something else. We must make him a non-human.

113

We must demote him from our own species into a species to be hunted and killed. This is by no means an inconsequential step. In fact, it is having to make this transition, having to precede our killing with something else, that keeps us alive today.

The examination of the football aggro phenomenon revealed a very important process. It showed that in the context of the striving for manly dominance a highly strategic weapon was the system of insults which served to demasculinize one's rivals. Making them appear homosexual or, better still, feminine was part and parcel of this particular manifestation of aggro. It was, in a sense, the limit to which degrading the opposition could be taken. It stopped short of the dehumanization process which, in the light of the implications of our hunting ancestry, seems to be a necessary requirement for killing. The point now comes when we are forced to look at the relationship between aggression and what I simply call the 'hunting factor'. What are the implications of living in a world where both of these human qualities are present?

The central thesis I have been proposing in this book is that aggression can be channelled, via the construction of certain social frameworks, into patterns of activity which pose only an illusory threat to the development and maintenance of what we take to be civilization. The hunting factor seems to pose more of a threat. We need to kill because we are flesh-eaters. It may even be that there are occasions on which we need to kill each other in order to redress some major imbalance that, for one reason or another, has come to threaten man's continued existence. But such occasions must, by necessity, be rare. Could it be that the social process which limits our readiness to dehumanize and to kill is very much related to that same process which is instrumental in ensuring that subduing one's rivals is not only a way of coping with aggression but also serves to prevent us reaching a point where we are able to legitimize the killing of other men?

Predictably, perhaps, I am going to suggest that this is indeed the case. I have been at pains to separate hunting and aggressive forces because I think they have quite separate origins and utilities. It is also the fact that this distinction has not been drawn at all clearly in the past that is at least partly responsible for the habitual failure to discriminate between quite distinctively different patterns of violent behaviour. Having made this distinction I now want to go on to argue that there is an interaction between aggression and the hunting factor. The two processes can come together under certain circumstances with quite horrific consequences. And they come together when the rival one is seeking to subdue is no longer a man –

he is a special kind of animal. Unlike other animals, however, he still poses a threat. He is a dangerous animal and he is also a rival. He must be deprived of his life for that, given this strangely anomalous state of affairs, is the only logical course to take. You can't enter into ceremonial conflict, into ritual aggro that involves the mutual acceptance of tacit rules of constraint, with a rival whose humanity you no longer recognize.

To realize the full horror of this situation we don't have to look very far. We have only to examine an event in recent history that stands out as an unhealed scar on the collective human consciousness – the systematic extermination of over 4,500,000 Jews and an untold number of gypsies and 'asocials' in the concentration camps of Nazi Germany.

It is very easy to assume that the German guards who packed men, women and children into the gas chambers of Auschwitz and Buchenwald were brutish maniacs – that they were true demons driven on by lust for slaughter and an insatiable need to kill. The reality, however, is very different. The whole business of mass extermination was carried out in a most methodical and thorough manner. The Jews, Gypsies, Russians, non-Germanized Poles, mental defectives and those simply defined as asocials were not subjected to the crazed attacks of foaming savages. They were marshalled into chambers, disguised with great precision as shower rooms, and without excitement poisoned or suffocated.

It is the precision and the lack of emotion in the whole affair that make it so horrific and frightening. How can a group of soldiers, living ostensibly normal lives, continue their everyday business and, at the same time, be responsible for herding thousands and thousands of human beings to their certain deaths. How could they watch as the *Sonderkommando*, recruited from among other prisoners trying to buy their own survival, clambered over the stiff blue corpses seeking out the valuables which had been secreted in inaccessible orifices of the bodies. And then to load this enormous mass of cold flesh and bone onto trolleys for disposal in open pits or crematoria. What ideal could be so high that such acts of total hellishness could be perpetrated in its name?

The frightening truth is that even these vile acts can be conducted with little concern once the targets, the innocent millions who died because of their race, their politics, or their handicaps, have been successfully reduced to sub-humans. If the naked, frail and starving figure before you is no longer a person but an animal or a non-human bag of bones, his death is of as little consequence as that of the poisoned rat or the vermin one crushes to extinction with ease, and even with enthusiasm. It is the conversion of men into non-persons, of women and children into mere pollutants, that enables these horrendous exterminations to take place. We can subject an entire rabbit population to the slow grisly death of myxomatosis with few protests being raised. After all, the rabbits eat the food in the fields, destroy crops and interfere with the management of our own basic resources. Once people have been converted into metaphorical rabbits their death is equally of little concern. How we kill them, and how they die is of only passing concern when they are seen as posing a threat to things like national progress and Aryan domination.

The hunting factor enables us to do things which would otherwise be unthinkable. It allows us to kill and to kill again. We can do it, other animals cannot and do not. We alone are mass murderers. But we are not killers because of some deep instinctive urge that drives us on to poison and burn each other. We kill because we alone are capable of making the vital symbolic transformation – the deadly conversion of our conspecifics into creatures of a totally different category. To a leopard, another leopard is a leopard is a leopard. He is unable to transform it into the kind of prey which he kills with ease to satisfy his hunger. Leopards can't make symbolic transformations. They may struggle for dominance or access to the best hunting areas, but they can't hunt each other. They can't use the lethal claws and teeth, which figure so prominently in their predatory behaviour, on each other. They must use some other equipment in their ritual fighting. It is man that can turn the full impact of his capacity and his equipment to kill towards his fellows. He can do this not because of his savage animal ancestry, but because he is a man. He alone can manipulate the symbols of the deadliest equation the world has ever known.

It is this uniquely human capacity of conceptualization and ability to endow objects, events, or people with particular kinds of images and meanings that sets man apart from other animals. It gives him the capacity to be a poet, a philosopher and an essentially creative and aesthetic creature. But this same gulf which separates him from even his nearest animal ancestors is also the one which endows him with the potential for his own self-destruction.

The symbolic endowing of candidates for the gas chambers with sub-human qualities is fairly well documented. We have only to browse through the Nazi propaganda of the 1930s and 1940s to see how easily a race of people can be held responsible for all of a society's ills and subsequently reduced to the status of a lesser breed. There are constant references to Jews as vermin and reptiles, as swine and filthy animals. There is also a lot made of their alleged animalistic behaviour. They were accused of eating their own children and of engaging in incest – both activities which a normal human would shrink away from. When men like Field-Marshal von Reichenau issued statements to his juniors such as ' . . . a soldier must have an understanding of the necessity of a severe but just revenge on sub-human Jewry', he was contributing to a process that served eventually to legitimize the enactment of 'The Final Solution'. He was also following very closely the guide lines laid down by the SS and known as the *Sprachregelungen*. These 'language rules' were a highly codified set of regulations concerning how the business of extermination and killing was to be described, and how the victims were to be labelled. It was a kind of sinister 'Newspeak' – a pattern of jargon which was to mask the sordid reality of what was going on inside the death camps and the gas chambers. The term 'Final Solution' itself was part of this bureaucratic cover-up. You can't live easily with words like 'liquidation' and 'mass extermination'. They arouse an immediate revulsion. But to speak of 'evacuation' and 'special treatment' makes life much more simple. Having removed the essential humanity of the victims, and having created a system of language which removes entirely the need for reactions of guilt and remorse, the machinery for achieving the ultimate in human destructiveness comes into being.

Herbert Kelman, the American social psychologist, has done more than most in revealing aspects of the whole dehumanizing process. His paper, 'Violence Without Moral Restraint', published in 1973, provides us with some very valuable concepts for seeing just how the business of turning people into non-people is accomplished. The symbolic transformation, it would seem, is not at all difficult to achieve because it relies on processes which are already available in the large-scale societies in which we now live. The social mechanics do not have to be specially constructed. The elements of the deadly equation are available to any power which cares to put them together. The elements Kelman called 'authorization' and 'routinization' are academic labels, indeed, but the processes themselves will be familiar to everyone.

Authorization is about obedience; about the fact that people will do a surprising range of things simply because they are told to by a person who is an authority figure. One of the most common defences at the Nuremburg trial was, of course, that those charged with committing acts of atrocity were simply following the orders of their superiors. The case of Lieutenant Calley in the My Lai trial also centred around whether or not he had been following a statutory obligation when he himself ordered the shooting of hundreds of innocent Vietnamese families. Obedience to those in authority seems to absolve a person from the responsibility for his own actions. After all, both the concentration camp commander and the army officer in Vietnam would argue quite convincingly that had he not done what was demanded of him, his fate would have been the same as that of his victims.

Obedience, however, does not rest solely on the prospect of retribution. It is something which follows automatically in the wake of the rather special authority relationships we find in our societies. Stanley Milgram, in a very elegant series of experiments, showed the frightening extent to which ordinary men and women are prepared to follow orders and commit acts they would normally find unthinkable.

If you walk out into the street and ask people if they would be prepared to give dangerous electric shocks to others their answer would be fairly predictable. 'No'. What Milgram did, however, was to invite paid volunteers to act as subjects in a psychological experiment. The object of the experiment was ostensibly to do with how people can be taught, or encouraged to learn certain tasks.

As each subject arrived he was led into a room with another person who, in fact, was a confederate of the experiment – a 'stooge'. Both the subject and the stooge drew lots to decide who was to be teacher and who the pupil. But the draw was rigged and the real subject always took the role of the teacher. The pupil, ostensibly just another subject, was put in a separate room, sat in a chair and had electrodes attached to him. The teacher sat in another room and in front of him was an alarming box with a dial calibrated from 'mild' to 'lethal'. This was the apparatus through which he was to deliver electric shocks to the pupil whenever he made a mistake in the task assigned to him. The shock was to be a kind of 'negative reinforcement': something which would speed up the learning process.

This may sound rather bizarre, but in fact a lot of experiments in psychology are conducted in just this way. Psychologists have a great passion for designing obtuse and bizarre experimental settings – a mania which derives from their ambition to be regarded as true scientists. Anybody who had even the slightest familiarity with psychological research of this type would have found little out of the ordinary in Milgram's laboratory. Except that is, for the calibrations on the dial. In Milgram's experiment, the box of tricks and the lever for delivering shocks were just dummies. At no point was the stooge to be electrocuted at all, but the pretence was well conducted. The teacher at his panel truly believed that the man next door, skilfully acting up when the lever was pressed, was really being caused considerable pain.

As the experiment progressed, the dial on the box was turned up until it went right up into the danger zone. Subjects protested a little. Some giggled nervously and some began to sweat profusely. But the majority went on. They went on because the experimenter, whose authority was unquestioned, assured them that everything was OK. Some went on pressing the lever even though they could no longer hear any of the anguished screams or the impassioned pleas that had accompanied each press of the lever before. Was he dead? They obeyed even when the dial read 400 volts!

These experimental subjects were just ordinary folk who probably had never once in their lives committed any noteworthy act of violence. They were not sadists, and electrocuting people was not something they would normally feel able to carry out. But when the electrocution – this rather insidious form of violence – is placed in a special context, they do it. They may feel bad about it but they do it, or at least they believe so. In a laboratory the relationship between the experimenter and his subject is fixed. The experimenter is an authority. He knows what he is doing and it is not part of the role of the subject to question the protocols. The fact that the laboratory is in a well-respected university, and not in a back alley, adds to the authority. 'They' wouldn't allow it to go on if it wasn't just so.

This disturbing zombie-like pattern of obedience is peculiarly human. People come to stand as figures of authority not because of their physical dominance but because of the symbolic status which is attached to them. The experimenter may appear as a rather insignificant little man. But because he wears a lab coat, or because he has even totally intangible badges of office, we do what he says in the laboratory. Elsewhere we might ignore him, but there he is a master.

If this is what can happen to ordinary folk when violence is legitimized through the authorization process, we can easily understand the fact that soldiers will, like robots, kill on command. The authority of senior officers is not something which can be challenged or made a subject for negotiation. There is, however, a very important limit to this process. The limit is reached when the acts one is required to carry out are seen as falling outside of the authority of the person who issues the commands. The subject in Milgram's experiments gives the shocks because they have a legitimate relationship to the reinforcement programme which is claimed to be the object of the study. If Milgram had asked his subjects to stand on

119

their heads or take off their clothes, their obedience would undoubtedly have been less automatic. Similarly even the soldier might baulk at being commanded to shoot at his own side. He might, quite rightly, decide that his officer's authority did not extend so far.

In Milgram's case, authority was seen to extend further than one might predict, because he assured his subjects that all was OK. The 'pupil' might cry out but subjects were told that the shocks were not harmful. To describe an act of extreme violence as not harmful introduces an added twist. People were faced with contradictory information. And that, presumably, is why they broke into a sweat or began to laugh in a very nervous fashion. The products of their acts were transformed, at least partly, into something else. They were obviously causing the man in the next room a lot of pain, but somehow this pain was not harmful.

The point here is that this kind of violence can only be enacted when not only is there a distinct recognition of authority but also when that authority succeeds in transforming the reality of the end-product of the violent acts. The process of authorization was clearly operating in Nazi Germany; it was the mechanism which enabled the ruling *élite* to operate their policy of 'purifying' an entire nation. But it was the more fundamental process of dehumanization which did the vital transforming of the outcomes of such a policy. Men followed orders because their orders came from legitimate authorities. The acts they were required to carry out were within the range of such authorities because what they were really doing had been symbolically changed. They were not killing fellow Germans or fellow men but rather giving 'special treatment' to things of a sub-human category.

The process of routinization sees to it that the link between dehumanization and authorization is maintained. If something is not human then to talk of murder would be inappropriate. A more neutral term must be given currency. An order to 'evacuate' a train packed with Jews is seen as a legitimate order. The translation from 'evacuation' into 'extermination' is rendered impossible by the acceptance of Jews as non-humans. And so the business proceeds. Authorization, routinization and dehumanization go hand in hand. Eventually the system gathers a sickening momentum of its own. The dehumanization of people leads to their treatment as animals. Witnessing people being treated as animals reinforces our belief that they are animals. Standing by the fence of Auschwitz, looking at those emaciated skeletons with shrunken skin and hollowed eyes – who could believe that these were really people? When people become dehumanized they begin to look and act sub-human. They can no longer fight back or attempt to change their image. They even begin to participate in their own dehumanization. The *Sonderkommando* had lost their ability to feel moral revulsion or to do anything other than pursue an animalistic fight to stay alive. The process of dehumanization is so effective that not only do people become firmly fixed with the sub-human symbol, they actually have their distinctive humanity removed from them.

The cycle of dehumanization, torture and killing, reduction of people to an animal-like existence, reaffirmation of the belief in the sub-human nature of these people – this sounds very familiar. It is in fact another example of a positive feedback loop. Dehumanizing people has consequences. These consequences lead to further dehumanization and very soon the loop is established. It is fixed until someone or something simply breaks it and interrupts the terrifying inertia.

There is one other sinister aspect of the dehumanization cycle. One which adds to the momentum it can ultimately gain. Kelman points it out very clearly:

> Continuing participation in the sanction of massacres not only increases the tendency to dehumanize the victim, but it also increases the dehumanization of the victimizer himself. Dehumanization of the victimizer is a gradual process that develops out of the act of victimization . . . . In sanctioned massacres, as the victimizer becomes increasingly dehumanized through the enactment of this role, moral restraints against murder are further weakened. To the extent he is dehumanized, he loses the capacity to act as a moral being.

What is happening here is quite fundamental and quite terrifying. Man is able to dehumanize others only because he, unlike animals, is able to make the vital symbolic transformation. Once the dehumanization cycle has started turning, however, he loses the only other human characteristic that might stop it. He loses the possibility of moral revulsion because he has lost that part of his humanity. Having used his human uniqueness to start the process he then abdicates part of this uniqueness. He becomes like the animal who can feel no remorse for the prey whose flesh he tears apart. Remorse is not in the animal's nature. Man escapes from nature, but in this case the very act of escaping is what enables him to return.

I have deliberately chosen to examine massacre and genocide because, by any criterion, these are the ultimate forms of violence man is capable of, short of total self-annihilation. I raised the subject of the processes which underlie these extremes because they are, I suggest, diametrically opposite to those which form the basis of aggro and the ceremonial resolution of conflict. The patterns of fighting between rival males which have appeared in all human societies throughout the entire history of our species are not ones which can ultimately lead up to the kinds of killing I have just been talking about. The two types of violence are not simply ends of the scale. They are not linked by a common dimension. They are fundamentally quite separate acts resting upon quite different processes. Aggro rests upon aggression – aggression which is the subject of social management. Massacres rest on the hunting factor and on the ability of our species to make people 'huntable'. Having said this, however, I want to suggest that the two processes do come together under certain circumstances. One such circumstance arises in the course of warfare.

Wars between rival tribes of Dani warriors are events which, as we have seen, are very much to do with male aggression and the search for dominance on the New Guinean plains. There is little in the way of any apparent motivation to engage in killing. The 'battle' is the thing – the love of combat and conflict. It is about making rivals retreat or submit, not about wiping them out. Such wars, however, are only possible among groups of people who have this essential tribal way of life. The tribe, the 'natural' living unit, contains a pattern of internal relationships which makes possible the direct social management of conflicts not only within the community but also in relation to other communities. In the case of the Yanamamö killing arises much more frequently because very serious issues of survival are involved. Their situation is, or at least was, extreme. But even here, warfare involves face-to-face confrontation. Weapons are used but they don't remove the necessity for involvement with one's enemies. Each side is required to meet the other. And among members of each side there is a vital cooperative bond. The two factors together add up to a natural system of control. In a nutshell, control is possible when the business of fighting remains doubly social.

Warfare today, on the other hand, is very different. In fact, as I suggested earlier, its nature has progressively changed as man has evolved from a tribal to a national species. The other major change has been that of increased technological sophistication in weaponry. The two radical developments mean that there is no longer the same degree of 'natural' management of conflict encounters. In addition, the changes which have led to the construction of large-scale groupings are just those which allow the process of authorization to be established. Having authorization means that individuals need no longer feel responsible for their own actions. This in turn means that killing becomes even more of a possibility. Whereas killing has never been a major outcome of aggression in the past, the aggressive process is potentially lethal. Subduing a rival can, in some cases, lead to death when ritualization is absent or is rendered inoperative. Take away social management and people will, indeed, kill and cause injury.

Wars arise out of man's new territoriality but, as we have seen, his territories are now very different from those of his ancestors. His territories, quite simply, contain too many people and cover too big an area. Territorial violations, when they arise in the pursuit of economic resources, lead to defensive reactions. Defence now is not something which can be largely ritualized. The outcomes are bloody.

It is at this point that aggression and the hunting factor are able to meet up with each other. The act of killing other men can, itself, be a dehumanizing event. The killing may arise because the social management of conflict is no longer effective, and this may arise for two reasons. Firstly, there may be so much at stake in a particular encounter that fights to the death are the only solution. Secondly, conflicts may become unmanageable simply because the social equipment at one's disposal is too unwieldy, impersonal or remote. When the management breaks down for this reason we are likely to find that the 'faulty' social system is also one which is tailor-made actively to encourage both the authorization and routinization processes which allow dehumanization to have its deadly consequences. In other words, we have an equation which enables a 'break-in' to the same feedback cycle which gave us Auschwitz and Belsen.

Killing, in the context of an impersonal relationship, leads to dehumanization because that is how the killing is legitimized. The fact that people have died, and the fact that their death is legitimate, leads us to conclude that they must have been less than human in the first place. How else could we live with the situation? The killing might not arise as a consequence of our having dehumanized the victim. But dehumanization can follow as a consequence of him being killed. A switch is thrown, and from then on violence takes on quite a different form.

The link-up between aggression and the hunting factor is only really possible in societies where warfare is conducted in a non-social manner. We happen to live in just such a society. Where warfare remains at a personal, face-to-face and distinctly social level, the consequences of killing are very different. You can't easily dehumanize someone with whom you have just shared a basically human encounter, even if you have killed him in the process. He is dead but he is a dead man. His death came from a trial of strength, a battle of wits – a set of values to which both protagonists subscribed. But once you have armies bigger than the size of a tribe, and once you have weapons which remove you from close contact and even sight of your enemy, then the situation changes dramatically. A whole new arena of violence opens up. Massacres such as that at My Lai become posssible.

What I'm suggesting in all this is that we can arrive at dehumanization and the equivalent of hunting behaviour in two ways. The first way is a direct one and arises out of pure economic consideration and issues of survival. Where physical survival is threatened (or at least seen to be threatened) and where the threat can be seen as coming from an identifiable sub-division of people within a society, then the elimination of the threat can be engineered through the symbolic transformation of that sub-division into non-people. The second route to hunting behaviour is, in a sense, accidental. It comes about when the management of aggression, arising out of a new territorialism, is uncontrolled to the extent that impersonal killings become routine events. The killings, in the context of special features of modern national groups, come to be legitimized through *post hoc* dehumanization. In both cases, though, the hunting factor gains its momentum only through the availability of large-scale social processes which are quite novel in terms of man's cultural evolution.

In one sense, this conclusion is similar to that drawn by Lionel Tiger and Robin Fox in *The Imperial Animal*:

> The human animal is hoist on its own cerebral petard. The brain that was good enough to produce the skilled hunter . . . was also good enough to produce huge empires, noble causes to die for, vast armies and megadeath.

Tiger and Fox, however, seem to see aggression and hunting as being very closely associated with each other from a very early point in our evolution, whereas I prefer to see the possibility of such an association arising for quite different reasons. Lionel Tiger, in particular, has argued that aggression in men is, in large part, a function of hunting. In the days of early *Homo sapiens* the requirements of survival demanded that men entered into cooperative bonds with each other in order to hunt for food most effectively.

That would seem to be indisputable. But hunting, I've suggested, is not, in any simple sense, the same as aggression. Nor are the two

124

necessarily related. We can see this difference very clearly in the behaviour of many species of hunting animals who have evolved very efficient and lethal tools with which to kill their prey. When those same animals engage in conflict encounters with their conspecifics, the deadly claws, teeth, horns and beaks are rarely brought into play. The bodily equipment, developed for the purposes of killing other animals, is reserved exclusively for that purpose. In fights concerning dominance or territory, what I take to be expressions of aggression in the proper sense, there are many cases where the ritualization process produces an almost bizarre pattern of behaviour in which the most effective equipment is concealed or kept out of the way. It isn't simply a matter of degree here. Ritualized aggression is not just a mild form of hunting behaviour – it is qualitatively different. And the fact that even totally non-hunting species resolve problems of aggression in much the same way as do their killer cousins, highlights the point even more.

When men enter into aggressive confrontations with each other, the object of the exercise is not killing but preservation of dominance relations, the defence of particular space or access to basic resources. In pursuit of these some killing may take place. But killing which arises out of a failure fully to manage aggression, and killing which arises out of hunting non-people, are radically different events. The biological association, for which Tiger and others argue very strongly, seems to be absent both in the world of animals and in what we might take, loosely, as being the 'natural' world of man. It's only when we get away from this natural world into the world of super powers and over-populated nations that an association begins to make itself felt.

The message here, I think, is clear. If we want to increase our understanding of man's continuing hostility to man through an examination of our evolution, then we must be very careful not to lump together patterns of behaviour which are quite different from each other. If we are interested in why men fight each other, then looking at how we evolved into a species which survived by killing animals is not a very logical line of inquiry to pursue – at least not in the beginning. Because even at a common-sense level we make a very strong separation between these two types of behaviour. The man who works in an abattoir, and who daily slaughters cattle, is not seen as a violent being. When Tory politicians or managing directors escape from the cities to shoot on the moors of Scotland, we don't accuse them of being aggressive tearaways. Equally, although we might not feel socially attracted to Big Game hunters, trappers or whalers, we would still be reluctant to put them in the same category as pub-fighters, gang leaders, and football hooligans. They are playing different games in different ball-parks.

The most obvious approach to the study of everyday aggression is to look at how men in societies, contemporary, historical and primitive, have actually engaged in it, what forms their fights have taken, how they have been managed, constrained and controlled, and what the outcomes have been. By contrasting this picture with that drawn from the studies of other animals, especially our nearest primate cousins, we can gain some clues concerning the origins of both the aggression process itself and its ritual containment. Only when we come to examine a quite different issue does the fact of man's hunting ancestry become directly relevant.

In suggesting that it is the loss of a tribal way of life which ultimately leads us to massacres, I'm also suggesting that Ardrey's hunting hypothesis is no more than that. It's a hypothesis for which I find little supporting evidence. His case, in fact, rests very heavily on the discovery of skeletons by Raymond Dart in South Africa of *Australopithecus africanus*, an early large-brained hominid. Many of the skeletons had skull fractures consistent with the idea that death had been caused violently and with weapons. From this finding he jumps to the conclusion that early hunting man was a savage murderer. But the jump is premature, and the link between killing and a hunting instinct is by no means a logical one. Even if these skeletons were of murdered men we have no reason to suppose that their murders were caused by the fact that hunting was the order of the day. That is the first mistake. Secondly, the evidence for murder is itself rather dubious. Montagu, for example, points out that the skull fractures are perfectly consistent with attacks by leopards. Leopards often go for the head when they attack their prey. They also have long canine teeth which make holes in heads remarkably similar to those in the skulls of *Australopithecus africanus*. And we know that there were leopards around the site where the skulls were discovered because their remains are also lying around in abundance. Who killed whom is anyone's guess here.

Apart from resting on very shaky foundations, the hunting hypothesis finds little comfort in the evidence of anthropology, ethology or contemporary social inquiry. To state that it is simply wrong or ill-conceived might be too unkind, but things don't look at all good for it. They look even worse when we turn to some very obvious examples of hunting communities, the North American Indians.

To the Plains Indian of America, hunting was a total way of life.

126

His whole existence centred upon the Buffalo and its food potential. He hunted it on foot and on horseback and the bow and arrow was the basic tool for survival. The tribes which made up the Plains population were nomadic, non-agricultural and were frequently in conflict with one another over who should have the right to hunt where. On the basis of Ardrey's hypothesis, this sounds disastrous. All the ingredients for killing and murder on a massive scale would appear to be present. But the story of the Sioux, Shoshone, Blackfoot, Apache, Comanche, and the other tribes of the Plains is not one of massacre and violent destruction. Not until, that is, the pioneers and frontiersmen arrived with the epithet that the only good Indian was a dead Indian.

War was as familiar to the North American Indians as to those in New Guinea. The ideals of the warrior and of male bravery were heavily embedded in traditional culture and life-style. But the warfare of these total hunters was still very ritualized. Colin Taylor, in *The Warriors of the Plains*, points out:

> Although Plains Indian culture was dominated by a martial spirit, continual warfare leading to extermination of a weaker group hardly finds a place in the annals of these warrior people . . . the necessity of observing strict rituals before the commencement of aggression was an effective means of establishing and maintaining tribal control over warfare.

Such conclusions are not drawn by Taylor on the basis of mere surmising and guesswork. His book is based, as far as I can see, on impeccable source material, including the ethnographies that were written at the beginning of the century using reliable and active tribesmen informants. What comes across most clearly is the fact that although the folklore and mythology which related to hunting became mixed up with that which was to do with fighting, wars were fought quite specifically against other *people*. Hunting and killing the buffalo was one thing – being a warrior was something quite separate.

The overlap between religious rituals associated with hunting and with war is shown up quite clearly in some of the war dances. Omaha warriors, for example, engaged in a very stylized 'wolf dance' before setting out on the war path. And part of the object of this dance, which imitated the animal's prowling footsteps, was the seeking of the wolf's predatory skills and powers. It's this kind of association which leads some people to conclude that hunting animals and fighting with men were both aspects of one general aggressive activity. But as Taylor again points out:

127

Uninitiated white men, who described war dances in blood lust terms, obviously completely failed to grasp the significance of what they were observing and the deep-seated cultural ethos of the People in which these ceremonies were embedded.

To the hunting peoples, the wolf was a powerful symbol of success. It had all the virtues for survival on the Plains – ones which tribesmen sought to emulate. And so we should hardly be surprised that the wolf appears as a central figure in mystical ceremonies, even those to do with war. Seeking predatory powers, however, was only one aspect of the war dance. Other qualities of the wolf, especially the ability to spend long periods alone and not be 'homesick', were ones which came much to the fore when warriors set out for a battle and required some 'dutch courage'.

Despite these conceptual confusions, the Omaha, for example, had a word for war which makes it quite clear that they distinguished it from all hunting activities. The word was *nuatathishon* and it meant, literally, 'war with men'. More particularly, it referred to fights with other adult male human beings – children and womenfolk were not considered legitimate targets of violent activities. Even the violence to be directed at other men was carefully circumscribed by a rigidly codified set of rules of conduct. The warrior did not set out to slaughter – he set out to win himself honour, glory and status. And simply killing a man from another tribe in war was a relatively inefficient way of achieving such accolades. In virtually all tribes the best way of winning fame was in 'counting coup'. Among the Omaha one did this by striking an unwounded enemy with the hand or with the bow. Some tribes had special 'coup sticks' for the purpose, but the principle was the same. You ran or rode up to an individual, gave him a totally non-injurious blow, and returned to your own ranks. In the process you risked your life. But since your enemy was also trying to count coup rather than kill you, the dangers were rather less than they might have been.

Killing an enemy, it must be said, did afford some honour, but the fact that killing was not the prime object of the exercise immediately puts warfare at a great distance from hunting. You wouldn't try to count coup on a buffalo. Nor would you gain great status from killing it. You would simply get fed. Male pride and a sense of aggressive achievement could be gained only in a quite separate sphere of tribal activity, and hunting, in contrast, was simply routine work. Hunting was undertaken in order to survive physically. War was undertaken because, partly, it ensured that a tribe could carry on hunting where it liked, but also as a means for social survival.

War honours were central in fixing and maintaining dominance hierarchies, for consolidating social and emotional bonds and for managing the aggression of male members of a tribe. And all this could be attained with very little killing and without anything in the way of dehumanizing violence.

A good deal of the hunting hypothesis has to do with the alleged inevitability of death and destruction following as a result of man's unique evolution as a weapon maker. But the North American Indians had very effective weapons. Their bows were, at least in the latter part of their history, much more efficient and accurate than even the early breech-loading guns. They were certainly far more useful than the old muzzle-loading equipment that the early white settlers shot things with. The bow was, of course, a logical development in hunting communities with unsophisticated technologies. With this weapon you needed no longer to rely on your ability to drive herds of buffalo over the edge of cliffs. You could stalk them, or better still, ride up to them on horseback and shoot them where they were. Equally one could now shoot other Indians with this tool. But the bow never evolved as a man-killing tool, neither was it subsequently modified to be maximally effective as such. Arrows, for example, had heads on them which were flat and pointed and made of flint. Later small triangular metal heads were used, often cut from things like frying pans bought from white traders. The heads were attached so that they were vertical, i.e., in line with the bow-string notch at the other end of the arrow shaft, and were designed to pass easily through the vertical ribs of the buffalo. In this role they were deadly. But men don't have vertical ribs – they have horizontal ones. So you would expect that if warriors were hell-bent on killing their enemies they would make a small modification to their arrows and rotate the heads so that they now lay at right angles to the string when fired. From the evidence of arrows collected from battlefields this modification seems not to have been made. The arrows, even with vertical heads, were still very dangerous. But killing buffalo was clearly seen as being far more important than killing rivals and an obvious opportunity for arms escalation was ignored.

This failure to make the most of available killing power is very reminiscent of the Dani's failure to put flights on their arrows. The Dani knew much about feathers and the North American Indians were very skilled in manufacturing arrow points. In both cases, however, there was a strong reluctance to direct the potential of such knowledge and craft towards their fellow men. They didn't do so because that would have run quite contrary to their perception of

129

warfare as being a game of prestige rather than a form of hunting in which the victims were men. The Dani, of course, were pig raisers and gardeners, but the Plains Indians, who were the archetypal hunters, fought each other with the same style and ceremony as that of their New Guinea cousins. The fact that hunting was a fully committed way of life had little impact on the mechanics of warfare, even though the symbols of predatory animals became enmeshed in the magical and mystical rites of the war dance. And, for me, this puts the lid on the hunting hypothesis – or at least on that part of it which insists that man's hostility to man, and the resolution of it, is bound up with his hunting origins. Yes, man has always killed for a living – but it is a long complicated journey from killing an animal to killing a man.

So I come back to the fundamental point that the move from killing animals to killing men is brought about through man's ability to manipulate symbols and to transform people into animals. He can also do the reverse, of course. He can be anthropomorphic and attribute to animals all sorts of human qualities – which is what devoted pet owners often do. In both cases, however, this ability to transform is something that we alone, as people, are able to do.

The hunting factor and man's new territoriality join forces in the bloody wars between nations. Ironically this pattern of warfare, and its devastating effect, comes about primarily because we gave up being hunters. We settled, domesticated our animals so that there was no need constantly to pursue them, built boundaries around our settlements, developed technologies which a nomadic people would have found impossible, and from there we grew. Our cultures expanded in size, and finally we achieved the very dubious honour of creating both the weapons of mass destruction and the social mechanisms which could legitimize their use. The starting point for all this, however, was not half a million or three million years ago, or in the South African caves of *Australopithecus africanus*. It was between five and ten thousand years ago on the banks of rivers and on the fertile plains where not only could animals graze but where wheat and beans could also be planted and harvested. That is ironic indeed.

The kinds of large-scale social changes I've been talking about – those which, I suggest, have been instrumental in making the hunting factor work against us – have produced changes not only in violence at a mass level but also changes at an individual and small group level. We are in the business of mass violence because we live in masses. And the pattern of this violence is brutal because we have little possibility of controlling it. But the fact that we live in masses

130

also makes it more difficult to manage aggression at an everyday level. In a sense, aggro can get lost in the cultural jungle we now call society. Aggression remains, no more and no less a force in man than before. But what we do with this process – how we reap its benefits and how we tame its sting – is something which does change. It is with this pattern of change, and the implications of it, that the next chapter is concerned.

7

Changing Patterns of Violence

Americans are great ones for appointing national commissions. There seems to be an ever-increasing trend in the United States towards investigating, in a formal and ponderous way, all things which make up the social condition. Little has escaped the attention of zealous bureaucrats and the respectable academics charged with boosting the pool of man's knowledge about himself. It's not very surprising, then, that Violence (with a capital V) became, in 1968, the topic which was to lead to a very impressive tome of epic proportions. The directors of the National Commission on the Causes and Prevention of Violence, appointed by President Johnson, were charged with the job of going 'as far as man's knowledge takes' in the pursuit of some explanation of why America seemed hell-bent on destroying itself from within. The published report, which emerged a year later, was 350,000 words long, contained twenty-two chapters and looked very impressive indeed. But all this, declared John Herbers in a special introduction to the volume, was probably insufficient to dispel a popular myth. The myth, so intractable as to be little affected by the workings of august government institutions, was spelled out succinctly by one of the Commission's directors, Ted Robert Gurr:

> Americans have always been given to a kind of historical amnesia that masks much of their turbulent past. Probably all nations share this tendency to sweeten memories of their past through collective repression, but Americans have probably magnified this process of selective recollection, owing to our historic vision of ourselves as a latter-day chosen people, a New Jerusalem.

Ted Gurr is clearly right, and perhaps it's too much to expect that this ostrich-like behaviour can be changed overnight by rational argument and intellectual persuasion. But Americans do not have a monopoly on such attitudes, nor are they alone in the stampede to set up committees of inquiry. The British are equally caught up in both the social myths and the love of official bodies. But whilst the myths are voiced with comparable volume, our government departments move more slowly. The Development Group of the Department of Health and Social Security began their study of violence after their American counterparts had already completed their work. And whereas the National Commission in the USA was able to produce 822 pages of published text in one year, the British DHSS took five years to produce a work of much more modest proportions – a mere 278 pages. There was, however, one very interesting thing in common between the two. Ted Gurr's claim for collective American amnesia was matched by John Rowbottom's assertion that, 'By contrast with many other nations the contemporary English have a very poor sense of their own history.'

Both reports insisted strongly that violence was firmly rooted in the past, that it was not simply the novel invention of a modern permissive society. As obvious as that may seem, it needed, and still needs, to be said. People forget, and in forgetting they cling to the dream that there have been happier times to which, one day, we might all return. But just as the Utopian future, like the rainbow, seems to retreat as you attempt to approach it, so the Utopias of yesterday often turn out, on more serious reflection, to have been just as bloody and just as problematic as the present. There is, however, an even more serious point to be made here. The editors of both the British and the American reports are right to insist on violence being seen in proper historical perspective. But when we open the covers of these books, what do we find? We find the American edition is neatly divided into sections such as 'The American Vigilante Tradition', 'Black Violence in the 20th Century', 'American Labor Violence' and so on. In the British report the structure is a little different, but there are still sections on 'Violence in Groups', 'Violence in the Media', 'The Violence within', etc. Both reports pay homage to a little psychological research and finally conclude that we still don't know very much about the subject – and that's true. But despite attempts at making distinctions between types of violence, the reports read as if aggro had never existed. There is virtually nothing on aggression management within informal social groups, very little on the positive aspects of hostile encounters, and only a token discussion concerning the nature and origins of human aggression. Only Geoffrey Pearson, with a chapter in the British report called 'In Defence of Hooliganism', comes anywhere near a slightly more positive approach. But he too loses his grip on rational thinking when he

133

concludes that hooliganism and the more ritualized forms of violence, such as 'blowing off steam at football matches', are to be taken simply as signs of increasing alienation. I wouldn't want to quarrel with the suggestion that football fans are becoming alienated – but there's a lot more to aggro than that.

The unconcern shown at this level of inquiry with the processes which underlie violence and hostility is quite alarming. There is a concern with history but not for seeing reflected in the past equivalents of a pattern of violence which we are now in danger of sending into oblivion. We are hastening its demise not through a conscious determination to wipe out ceremonial forms of conflict resolution, but because we no longer recognize that they are different from the patterns of violence which pose real, rather than imaginary, threats to our societies. At one time, I believe, we did accept that some aspects of violent behaviour were socially acceptable – even useful. We encouraged boys at their 'fisticuffs'. We learned to live with the Byzantine bovver boys, because we felt that this machismo business was better acted out at the circus than in the more sensitive and less tangible arenas of political and social life. We applauded the knights on their chargers and the values to which they subscribed. Today the blinkers are down and we can see only death, destruction and disorder. We are blind to ritual and to the swinging fist which just fails to connect with anything.

Now this might sound rather like the nostalgia I was previously decrying. Perhaps I, too, am caught up in a parallel hysteria, and perhaps the predecessors of our football hooligans have always been misunderstood. But what I want to argue is that whilst the forms of violence in our societies today are as old as the hills, two things have changed. Firstly, the ability to express collective outrage has increased in proportion to the availability of channels of communication. Secondly, the overall pattern of violence has changed in the sense that there has been a shift in the balance between highly injurious instrumental violence and relatively less injurious non-instrumental violence. This shift is the product of a radical change in the kinds of society in which we now live. The question I want to address is not 'Why is man becoming more violent?' but rather 'Why is man's violence becoming different?' To get to a point where it might be possible to throw up some answers to the second question, I'd like to offer some reasons for believing that the first is a non-issue.

Those who protest most loudly about increasing violence in our societies are usually those who are able to marshal very impressive-looking statistics to support their case. Graphs relating to crimes of violence rocket upwards; the figures, it is suggested, speak for themselves. But numbers have no voice of their own. They need to be interpreted and made sense of. It's often said that statistics can be made to prove anything you like. That I don't believe, but statistics can be misused and can be the basis of very misleading conclusions. So a small diversion into the world of arithmetic and collection of numbers is called for. And the first problem is that of defining the thing to which numbers relate. I'd like to start with a cautionary tale.

Some years ago I attended a lecture given by an eminent British psychiatrist. His theme was a comparative analysis of the incidence of schizophrenia in various national populations. He took the view that this particular form of mental illness had a biochemical basis to it and was relatively unaffected by social conditions, family life or childhood experiences. To support this rather bold assertion he recounted how he had gone on a 'diagnostic expedition' to a small Carribean Island where no white psychiatrist had ever set foot before. And lo and behold! he found that the proportion of the population suffering from schizophrenia was about the same as in Britain. Now all sorts of objections can be levelled at such superficial and theoretically vacuous approaches to mental illness, but that is not the point of the story. The point is about this notion of statistical proportion. Before the psychiatrist set out on his trip there was no statistic. We didn't know how many schizophrenics there were on this Island. But when the data had been analysed a number suddenly appeared. It said that X per cent of the population were mad. But nothing changed. Local people went about their everyday business in the same way that they had done before. The people who were allegedly insane had not gone mad overnight. In fact, few people had noticed that there was very much wrong with them.

The moral here is that statistics exist because people like collecting them. And when there appears to be some change in the statistics, that can mean at least three things. Firstly, it can suggest that there has been some change in the ways in which people behave. Secondly, it can mean that there has been a change in the ways in which we define what people do. Thirdly, it can suggest that the manner in which we assemble data and arrive at our statistic is different from some earlier procedure. I'm not entering into a debate just yet about how we draw inferences from statistics. I'll come to that in a moment. I'm taking the issue at a much more basic level and suggesting that what we take to be facts can be something quite different.

If you look at the figures relating to crimes of violence in the family you find something very striking. More and more men are appearing before the courts charged with physically assaulting their wives. Battered wives suddenly become the focus for collective concern, and shock is expressed at the fact that this particularly unsavoury form of violence is on the increase. But in all probability it isn't. All that is happening is that wife-beating increasingly is coming to the attention of the law enforcement agencies, and that is a very different thing altogether. In times past it was considered an almost inalienable right of an aggrieved husband to enforce what physical punishment he thought fit on his wife and, even more so, on his children. It is not so long ago that wives were literally the property of their spouses and were treated as such in even quite liberal and enlightened households. As husband-wife relationships have changed both in law and, to perhaps a lesser extent, in real human and social terms, men punching their women in the teeth after a skin-full at the local pub on a Saturday night have become less tolerated. New values have partly replaced the old to the extent that what was once unremarkable and inconsequential is now the subject of moral sanction and reproach. In other words, here our statistic indicates not a change in the levels of intra-family violence, but rather a decline in the toleration of such violence. Wives feel able to report their beatings to social workers and the police. Battered-wives refuges open to offer women some way out of intolerable family situations. The whole business suddenly becomes visible. And by being visible it becomes the subject for even more concern. The concern leads us to seek more and more prosecutions against violent husbands. The graph shoots up off the top of the page.

The point is, perhaps, an obvious one. But both in Britain and America we are bedevilled by people (and social scientists are not excluded) who would have us believe that the available data indicate a steady progression toward more violence, more crime and more misery. As James Q. Wilson put it:

> People who complain about 'crime in the streets' are prone to draw from crude crime statistics the conclusion that America is, morally, going to hell in a handbasket. It is important, therefore, to demonstrate that, statistically, we are a long way from hell, and in fact may not be in that particular handbasket. ('Crime in the Streets')

Wilson's critique of official statistics, whilst now a little dated, is still very relevant. He goes on to point out that although we might be aware that statistics are inadequate and misleading in this area, and

although we might insist on caution when making interpretations, we are still taken in by them.

Even the social scientists who write articles demonstrating that
the alleged 'crime wave' is a statistical illusion or simple myth
are likely to tell their wives (or even themselves) that, if they
live near such big-city universities as Chicago, Columbia, or
Pennsylvania, they should not walk the streets alone after dark.

Although we might, at a rational level, question the accuracy and
the relevance of statistical material, we still get caught out by our
feelings of horror and revulsion at what might seem to be happening
in our streets and neighbourhoods. It's this schizoid approach which
I take as being indicative of our current fascination with violence.
The statistics may be equivocal, but if we want to believe that our
fellow men are rapidly mutating into savage killers or, in contrast,
that men are naturally passive and gentle folk, then caution is likely
to be thrown away. The inferences we draw from the raw numbers
will often be directly to do with the 'facts' we want to find rather
than with a genuine concern for balanced explanations. And this
can lead to quite nonsensical debates among people who, one might
think, should know better. An example of this nonsense crops up in
the comparison of levels of violence in different cultures.

Robin Fox, in his book *Encounter with Anthropology,* makes the
point that there is no evidence to support the notion of totally
non-violent human societies.

Pueblo Indians, Eskimos, Bushmen, have all been cited as
examples of non-violent people, and all turn out to have high
rates of personal violence. The Bushmen of the Kalahari
Desert, it turns out, have a higher homicide rate than Chicago!
A book was written about them called *The Harmless People,*
which only goes to show that while anthropologists might be
nice folk who like to think well of their fellow men, they can be
poor guides to reality.

Now Robin Fox gives no figures to support such a claim, and one
might even question whether Elizabeth Thomas, who wrote *The
Harmless People,* could rightly be classed as an anthropologist.
Ashley Montagu, however, in *The Nature of Human Aggression*
makes a savage attack on what he sees as Fox's outrageous slur on
the Bushmen's character which leads to number-rigging of a quite
astonishing kind. Montagu himself quotes Richard Lee's field study
of the Bushmen in which he found that between 1920 and 1969
there were a total of twenty-two deaths arising out of violent

encounters among tribesmen. The average population of the !Kung Bushmen was about 1,300, giving a homicide rate of 34.5 per 100,000 per year (which is the normal way of expressing such a statistic). Now if one refers to the homicide figures collected by the Department of Health, Education and Welfare in America, we find that over the same period the homicide rate in the United States was about 7 per 100,000, the peak coming in the late 1930s when the rate rose to 10 per 100,000. This figure is uncomfortably high. It is, for example, ten times as high as the rate for England and Wales over that period – but it is still only a fifth of the Bushmen's level of homicide. So how is Montagu able to say that 'the Bushmen were and are rarely homicidal.'? Quite simply, he enters into a flight of fantasy that leaves one almost breathless:

> If one compares this with the US homicide rate, and takes into consideration the fact that in the United States many people recover from attempts on their lives owing to superior medical care, that large numbers of attempted homicides go unreported or are attributed to other causes, that many deliberate homicides are caused by means that are never recognized, to which one may add deaths caused by American intervention in the affairs of foreign nations, then the comparable American homicide rate rises to *about 100 per 100,000 of the population* (my italics).

Suddenly a figure of 7 has been changed to 100 simply on the basis of Montagu's dislike of the comparison that Fox is trying to make. It may be that comparing homicide rates in this manner is not the best way of tackling the issue. But to simply argue that one side, and only one side, of the equation has something wrong with it solves nothing. Bringing in totally irrelevant points such as the fact that medical care is better in America than in the Kalahari Desert is just a deliberate attempt to confuse the issue. Robin Fox is not talking about attempted murder, and if he were, one might find that in a culture without sophisticated arms and Saturday Night Specials the proportion of attempts to fatalities might be considerably higher. All one can deduce from Montagu's diatribe is firstly, that he is blind to the fact that violence exists even in apparently peaceful communities, and secondly, that he can't tell a proper statistical argument from a hole in the road.

One other point remains to be made about the use of numbers. It's quite clear that the numbers themselves can be the subject of all manner of questioning. They might under-reflect the incidence of a particular form of violence because such violence does not always come to the attention of data collectors. Equally apparent changes in numbers over time might reflect nothing more than changes in the degree of visibility. But even if we can somehow manage to compensate for all this there is still another hurdle to be crossed. What do changes and statistical trends mean and what causes them?

The standard way of addressing this problem in the social sciences is to make use of correlations. We try to find other things which are associated with changes in particular social phenomena. Thus we might find that violence increases in proportion to urban over-crowding, loss of recreation, breakdown of family units, and so on. On the basis of the discovered correlations we might go on to say that the increase in violence is caused by such factors. But here another cautionary tale is called for.

One of the most impressive correlations I have come across in recent years in Britain is that between the rise in the average age at which people die and the number of miles of motorway that have been opened. People live longer in direct proportion to the increasing availability of ribbons of concrete running all over the country. The facts here are indisputable. But would we feel confident in running an advertising campaign along the lines of the M1 being good for one's health? Probably not. There is indeed a very strong correlation here but a total absence of any direct causal link. Rather both factors are a product of something like our increasing technological sophistication which manifests itself equally in medical care and in rapid concrete construction methods. So the moral of this particular tale is that the link between two correlated social features might often have to be found elsewhere in society and at a more fundamental level.

Statistics-bashing is an easy game to play, but after a while it becomes rather unfruitful. Points need to be made about the gross misuse of numbers, but eventually you have to come up with something a bit more positive. The changes which everyone imagines are taking place may exist more in statistical practices than in the real social world, but I want to go on and suggest that there are some changes in the modes and patterns of violence which the statistical methods are too insensitive to detect. Whilst the levels of violence may rise or fall only slightly through history (with a few notable peaks and troughs), patterns of violence might change much more rapidly and often quite remarkably. In pursuing this argument, much of what I have to say is, by necessity, rather speculative. Statistics are of little use here because offences in the statute books make little distinction between forms of violent behaviour other than in terms of the severity of their outcomes. More importantly, it is only quite recently that we have come to regard some patterns of conflict as offences at all. Only the social scientist with a research grant big enough to buy him a personal time-machine would be able to gather the data required for an empirical analysis in this domain. But all is not lost. History, as we've seen, has not gone unrecorded and ideas are not a bad alternative to cold statistics.

In the last chapter I tried to make a very simple point. I suggested that on the basis of historical evidence, the aggro on the football terraces and on the street corner had a very long pedigree. Although our past has been as violent as our present, there has always been the characteristic pattern of conflict resolution among men and boys that I have taken to be analogous, in some respects at least, to ritualized aggression in animals. Associated with such rituals have been social attitudes which afforded them considerable tolerance and even positive encouragement. People sometimes became incensed when things got out of hand, but by and large the whole male dominance/aggression business was accepted as part of normal everyday life. That, however, is no longer the case. Aggro remains, at least in Britain, but it's becoming fragile. Its fragility is evidenced by the panic which surrounds it and which could ultimately destroy it. And as aggro begins to play a less central role in the management of aggression we bear witness to an increase in forms of violence which are much more a cause for genuine concern. Once we lose the ability to channel aggression into 'safe' outcomes, we are in trouble. In fact, I believe we're in trouble already.

It's ironic that our society should now be responsible for aggression becoming less managed through attempts to manage it too much. But that is what has happened. Our modern society is founded upon interference in people's lives. That, in itself, is not to be condemned because that is what social responsibility is all about. Nobody ever achieved anything like a just society by leaving people alone, and the concept of *laissez faire* has never brought nearer the day of revolution. But interference of any kind produces its own special set of consequences. If such consequences become caught up in positive feedback cycles of the kind I've discussed in earlier chapters then what might be seen as the noblest of actions can have very serious repercussions for the future of a society.

What has happened, I believe, is that our interference in people's expression of aggression has been misguided to say the least. Unlike our ancestors, even fairly recent ones, we accept unequivocally the idea that violence is something we must eradicate. Instead of looking for ways of socializing it we stamp on it. In fact we violently stamp on it and then wonder why it hits back. We can't accept that there are forms of violence we have to live with for the precise reason that our societies remain founded upon the need for aggression.

Bruno Bettelheim, a man for whom I have a great deal of admiration, is repulsed by violence. Yet he remains able to see that simple revulsion is hardly a substitute for rational thinking and making a determined effort to come to grips with the subject. In a paper called 'Violence: A Neglected Mode of Behaviour' he makes perhaps unnecessary references to instincts and simplistic genetic theories, but his conclusions are unquestionably appropriate ones.

> What I believe is needed . . . is an intelligent recognition of 'the nature of the beast'. We shall not be able to deal intelligently with violence unless we are first ready to see it as part of human nature, until we have gotten so well acquainted with it, by learning to live with it, that through a slow and tenuous process we may one day domesticate it successfully. In short, we cannot say that because violence *should* not exist, we might as well proceed as if it did not.

Bruno Bettelheim ends his paper by suggesting that the ultimate in domestication will come when we have learned to channel aggression into forceful expressions which are totally non-violent. In a moment I'm going to suggest that this is asking too much, if in talking about non-violence he excludes the pattern of violence which doesn't hurt very much. But at least there is a will to move towards working with violence rather than against it in the hope that one day its bloody potential will be tamed through understanding.

Working to eradicate, rather than to socially control, violence leads to changes we can actually see. It changed, for example, what the Teddy Boys did. Everywhere they went they were hounded by the police, traders, cinema owners and the media. Eventually they drifted into the alienated violence associated with attacks on black members of their communities. I'm not, for one moment, suggesting that the rise of racial conflict is due solely to our efforts at destroying aggro. But when social and political forces move us in that direction, the absence of opportunities for ritualized violence increases the likelihood of young men turning their aggression and their feelings of being downtrodden against handy minority groups.

An additional consequence of suppressing group aggro is the destruction of the groups and micro-societies in which ritualized aggression is acted out. And this, in turn, gives rise to some very serious consequences. Because in the kinds of society in which we

141

now live, micro-societies have a very fundamental role to play. In a very real sense, the existence of micro-cultures reflects a turning back to a very primitive way of living. As I've suggested, belonging to a group of soccer bovver boys is like being a tribesman. The fan, at least on Saturday afternoons, can feel part of a real social entity – one in which there are common values, shared meanings and well-understood aims. And that is not something available to him in the weekday world of school or work. Only on the terraces, in his tribe, can he achieve the things denied him everywhere else.

In clamping down on informal social institutions we move even further away from the values once associated with a far more natural way of life. The fan doesn't live in a tribe but, very probably, on a far from perfect housing estate. But the ideals he shares with his mates at weekends are tribal indeed. As the possibility of this kind of sharing becomes remote, our society moves even more inexorably towards anonymity and estrangement. The effect of this is to increase still further our inability to recognize the social function that aggro plays. In the light of social change, aggro appears anomalous and foreign. So we decry it even further, break up more forcibly the groups of people who engage in it; a familiar cycle. Without micro-cultures in which to express aggression, young males look elsewhere. But now the arenas have gone, and along with them the rules and constraints – the vital rituals. The expression of aggression becomes far more unpredictable. At the extreme it becomes random and gratuitous. Anarchy is the price you pay for destroying order.

This kind of change which, put very crudely, might be summarized as a drift from 'good' violence to 'bad' violence, is in fact lurking around in those statistics I was at pains to warn against. The problems of interpretation remain, but we can still draw some illumination from them. I don't want to sound unduly alarmist here. We have to remember that in these allegedly violent times in Britain far more people die as a result of motor-car accidents than from the deliberate violence of their fellow men. In fact, more people kill themselves than are killed by another person. And between a third and a half of all homicides are committed by people classed as insane. But it is when you start looking at levels of violent behaviour such as that involved in the offence of causing 'grievous bodily harm' that you begin to notice some changes. In 1945, malicious woundings accounted for 57 per cent of all offences against the person in England and Wales. In 1967 the proportion was 88 per cent, and in addition the total volume of offences against the person rose from 4,743 to 41,088, an increase of 766 per cent. Figures for the period after 1970 reveal a similar trend. Even treating these figures with extreme caution, and bearing in mind all possible sources of distortion, they still look significant. What they reflect, I suggest, is not that people fight each other more, but rather that fights now have far more serious consequences. Men are about as aggressive as they always were, but aggression, as its expression becomes less orderly, has more blood as its consequence.

One very important thing to note about these figures is that soccer hooligans, and their predecessors, have made but a tiny contribution to the totals. Serious injuries on the football terraces have been as rare as those on the South Coast beaches or in the cinemas and dance halls of the 1950s. Things like malicious woundings occur elsewhere, and their frequency increases in step with the loss of opportunity for social fighting.

In the United States, where there is more of everything and everything is bigger, criminal statistics look rather nasty when compared with the British ones. But again, some very exaggerated claims are made concerning the extent of violence in America. Ashley Montagu, we have noted, is an offender in this area but he is not alone. Jeffrey Goldstein, in *Aggressions and Crimes of Violence,* does some equally tricky number juggling. He states, for example: 'For the United States as a whole, the homicide rate (homicides per 100,000 population) is . . . 23 times that of . . . England and Wales . . .' That's on page 119. Earlier in the book, however (on page 83 in fact), he gives a very neat table showing the homicide rates for thirteen different countries. Here, we find that the American rate is given as 6.1 and the English rate as 0.7. A little simple arithmetic tells us that, according to these figures, the US homicide rate is 8.7 times the British rate. This, in fact, is the correct ratio. The ratio of twenty-three is a fiction derived, it seems, from sources such as the *New York Post* and the *Philadelphia Inquirer* – not the most reliable of guides compared with the US Government Printing Office's publications.

Even a factor of around nine is, of course, still a big difference. But homicides alone are not a very good guide to differences in the patterns of violence in a particular society. They don't tell us much about everyday events in which people come into hostile conflict with each other. Other statistics do, nevertheless, give us some clues concerning a very marked difference in one aspect of violence in both the USA and Britain – that is its instrumentality. Instrumental violence is that which is used in the pursuit of some direct material gain. When we compare figures for crimes such as robbery in the two countries a ratio of something in the region of 100–150

143

emerges, and a similar ratio is reflected in other statistics relating to lesser crimes. In other words, violence seems to be very much more a means to a specific end in America than it is in Britain, and that is a difference even more fundamental than the one shown up by the homicide rates.

There is, however, an even more important point to be drawn from this. Out of all the robberies which are classed by the FBI as strong arm – that is robberies involving physical force but no weapon – about 37 per cent are what people now refer to as 'muggings'. Muggings also account for about a quarter of all robberies involving a knife, club or other non-fire-arm weapons. Morton Hunt points out in his book *The Mugging* that these figures are probably very conservative:

> ... the term 'mugging' is also applied to that small but unknown fraction of the 330,000 reported aggravated assaults in which robbery was intended but not consummated, and to a fair number of felony murders (which make up more than one fifth of all homicides), in which the intended robbery leads to unintended death.

In fact, Morton Hunt suggests, the chances of being the victim of a mugging if you live in a major American urban environment are between 1 in 260 and 1 in 340. Now mugging is clearly instrumental, but the end-product is trivial. The average yield from a mugging is less than $5, and the violence involved is often far in excess of that needed to steal a wallet or a handbag. The theft, in other words, is almost incidental – it simply provides a focus for violent activity – and its impact on a society is catastrophic. This effect, eloquently drawn by Morton Hunt, is one which reflects the ultimate non-social expression of aggression:

> ... what alarms us and most gravely damages our faith in our society is the ever present threat of some sudden, unpredictable, savage assault upon our own body by a stranger – a faceless, nameless, fleet-footed figure who leaps from the shadows, strikes at us with his fists, an iron pipe, or a switchblade knife, and then vanishes into an alley with our wallet or purse, leaving us broken and bleeding on the sidewalk. Headlines are made of riots, rapes, dope-smuggling, embezzlement, while the mugging – ironically simple in execution and trifling in yield – is relegated to inside pages or ignored altogether; yet it is this, rather than the more complex and newsworthy crimes, that is responsible for the flight of millions of Americans to the

suburbs, the nightly self-imprisonment of other millions behind locked doors and barred windows, and the mounting attacks of law-and-order advocates upon constitutionally guaranteed rights that are fundamental to our concept of democracy.

That, for me, is the clearest statement about the dangers of losing socially controlled expressions of aggression. The damage is done not so much by the violence itself but rather by the manner in which the violence is enacted. Folk are not afraid of motor cars despite the fact that they are far more deadly and injurious than muggers. What is so frightening is the random impersonality of it all. A couple of young men get together, decide to 'pull a score', and an unknown stranger lies bleeding on the pavement. They do it not for the money but from frustration and alienation. The aggression is there – living in American society sees to that – but there's nowhere for it to go.

It is towards the pattern of violence, which finds definition in mugging, that I believe the British male is beginning to move. It's not that he is becoming more murderous in his activity, nor is he just becoming more acquisitive in his violence. Instead he is becoming more and more like his American counterpart who uses the opportunity to rob as a rationale for gratuitous attacks. He shows up in the statistics, but the numbers never quite spell out what the real danger is, nor how it comes to figure more prominently in our society. We assume, quite wrongly, that it is the aggro boys who are swelling the court lists and who are basically no different from the youths who cosh people on the heads late at night in dark alleys or even on the brightly lit streets. And by being increasingly wrong England moves closer to America.

The transatlantic comparisons of this nature provide us with the ultimate cautionary tale. The others are mere asides in comparison. America doesn't occupy the pride of place in the homicide stakes – Mexico, Nicaragua, Venezuela, Sri Lanka, Kuwait and Taiwan are all higher in this league. It just lacks much in the way of specific arenas for aggro. Only within the street-corner gang culture do the values and patterns of behaviour central to the social ritualization of aggression manifest themselves. Here the idea of 'rep', with its emphasis on masculine toughness, is very marked and fights between rival gangs are often stylized, ceremonial and relatively bloodless. But the sub-cultural framework which surrounds these activities is both too weak and inappropriate for the satisfactory management of aggression to be achieved. The gang fight is not, in fact, a central activity. It is peripheral to other exploits such as shoplifting, pocket-book theft and, indeed, mugging – features which have been far less salient in equivalent European groups. The danger is clearly spelt out. Where aggro is, at best, a fringe activity, the predominant pattern of violence poses an almost incalculable threat because of its essentially asocial nature. In cultures where there exist possibilities for expressing aggression in an orderly manner, where social attitudes do not lead to ridiculous censure and repression and where distinctive arenas for ritual displays flourish, the overall pattern of violence is very different.

This difference in patterns of violence cannot be explained simply in terms of corresponding differences in affluence and technological sophistication. In Sweden, for example, the standard of living is extremely high and technology abounds. But so do the *raggare* and the *knutters*. They ride around Stockholm, get into fights, and upset people. Gratuitous attacks on unknown victims, however, are not part of their social order. They are much closer to Parisian adolescent street gangs, *blousons noirs* and, more recently, *'les Punks'* – who tend to be rather more energetic than their British New Wave contemporaries. The Germans too, for all their dedication to national progress and materialism still retain within their youth cultures many of the traditional values associated with the resolution of male conflicts and slights of honour. And the beer cellar is just the place to enact such rituals.

The Italians, of course, have special social tools at their disposal for settling disputes without bloodshed. They are called gestures. The young subscriber to the cult of machismo in Naples is able to settle affairs of honour and dominance without speaking and without even leaving the seating of his Alfa Romeo. A 'fight' between two Italians – something which is more likely to result from scratched paintwork than a quarrel over a girl – often consists of little more than a frenzied exchange of hand signals and ritual posturing. The idea is not so much to hurt one's opponent but rather to dazzle him into retreat.

Another very clear example of this pattern of aggressive activity is to found on Tory Island, a Gaelic speaking community off the coast of Ireland. Robin Fox, in 'The Inherent Rules of Violence', gives an amusing account of 'fights' among these rural Irishmen which usually take place outside of the community's only church hall. Protagonists enter into long and involved exchanges of insults and threats but rarely ever come to blows. 'Hold me back or I'll kill him' is a typical phrase. And the aggressor will usually insist that his friends or relatives do, in fact, hold him back. Indeed, Fox remarks, one can often be forgiven for thinking that the fight is not between the two principals but between each and his holders. For a fighter to take off his coat would be a serious escalation of the whole affair. Thus, one often witnesses a lengthy ritual in which the holders struggle to prevent the fighters from removing their arms from their jacket sleeves. Only under very exceptional cases are any injuries sustained. The social framework in which the fights take place, and in which the kith and kin of each protagonist have well-understood roles, makes for an almost absurdly safe ceremony. The lads can 'have a go' at each other with only minimal risk of physical damage.

The comparison I'm making is not simply between football bovver boys and New York hoodlums. It's between methods of coping with aggression which have, in the past at least, been worlds apart. The gulf, however, is shrinking, and in Britain the change is becoming most noticeable. Rural Gaelic folk on Tory Island may still be reluctant to 'take off their coats'. But the British teenager is an easier prey to what has been aptly called the 'Coca-Cola syndrome'. He watches American TV programmes, speaks almost the same language and lives in a society where attitudes change fast. His elders have developed an aversion to aggression which is matched only by the Victorians' apparent horror of sex. The images of violence now churned out in ever-increasing quantities in films, on TV and in the papers probably serve the same limited function that prostitution did in the nineteenth century. But repression, rather than management, of aggression can have far more serious consequences in social terms than the suppression of sexuality. There's no aggressive equivalent of masturbation. And watching violence portrayed on a screen is no more satisfactory than reading pornographic magazines. Repression of overt aggressive expression, coupled with a continued transmission of the aggression process as a central feature of our social fabric, is a recipe for a very immediate kind of cultural disaster – a serious shift in the balance between categories of violence.

8
Epilogue
The Future for Aggressive Man

To say that we now face the most critical turning point in the history of the world sounds melodramatic in the extreme. But never before has man had the potential to commit the ultimate act of violence – the destruction of every living organism on his planet. Desmond Morris in *The Naked Ape* glumly suggests that by the end of the century we might all be dead, victims of the final nuclear holocaust. Our only consolation will be the fact that as a species we have had an exciting term of office.

On the available evidence, his case seems well founded. And the conclusions I've been drawing in the last few chapters might appear to lend weight to this thesis of despair. But having looked at the dangers we face as patterns of violence change within our societies, I want to end on a more optimistic note. The optimism is possible only because I believe that despite our technological and social sophistication we have not quite reached the point where the lessons of nature are entirely meaningless.

I've suggested that we are facing a crisis which centres on our increasing failure to manage aggression. And this has come about not because we are natural slayers of our fellow men but because we alone have been able to put a special kind of divide between ourselves and our evolutionary roots. We can no longer rely on nature to help us in the way that lizards can. We have to create and maintain social solutions instead. Now the chimp has this problem too. Little of his behaviour is instinctive in any simple sense. But he and other primates can never distance themselves from their biological heritage in quite the same way. And there's a very simple reason for this. Despite the attempts of a few gifted animal behaviourists to teach chimps sign language, it is clear that they are unable to communicate in a purely symbolic and abstract fashion. People can, and that makes all the difference. In some ways it helps us to develop social rituals for the containment and safe expression of aggression. Instead of being limited to the use of restricted components

148

of fighting behaviour, like fist waving, to express our hostility, we can go one stage further. We can call our rivals 'wankers' or use our linguistic skills to achieve even more effective put-downs. On the other hand, it is this same unique skill of concept management and expression which enables us to transform our fellow humans into non-humans – into a category which allows us to hunt and to exterminate them. And when our societies become unbalanced and impersonal, when power and authority are remote and when the cultural forces so central within tribes are no longer in evidence, we do so with alarming efficiency. Tribal values, however, never seem to vanish for good. They can be lost during social and economic upheavals, but they come back. And it's because of this that our potential for survival is increased. Ironically, it's the aggro boys – leading champions of tribal values – who can give a considerable boost to this potential.

On their own, the exponents of aggro in contemporary society cannot be expected to provide a panacea nor, at a stroke, guarantee the future of civilization. Ritual solutions of conflict, although basic elements of human social behaviour, cannot withstand the full force of a society's misguided struggle to eradicate them. In this sense, aggro is fragile. It has been endlessly transmitted and reproduced through evolution and through cultural development, but today we have achieved the social means of effecting its demise. At the same time, however, things are happening which might prevent us from going too far in this direction. Tribal values are being reintroduced not only on the soccer terraces and their equivalents but also, in a less dramatic way, in quite different areas of social life.

The idea of the commune for example gained most active support in the USA, and hippies emigrated from the urban concrete wastes to live in villages of junk architecture and geodesic domes. The concepts of sharing and of group order were reintroduced into a nation which seemed almost to have abandoned them in its greedy pursuit of material affluence. Awareness of the relationship between man and his world has also been re-awoken as our planet has been steadily plundered of its life-sustaining resources. The Maring cut-and-burn and go to war and the forest survives to support them. Western man forgets to care for his forest but, just in time, he invents ecology. A slow process of repair begins. Steps are taken to control pollution, the use of fossil fuels and the hazards of nuclear power. We begin to look again for alternatives to advanced technology – to the sun, the wind and the sea. When our production of food becomes so wasteful of natural resources and potentials, when we extract so many vital vitamins from it that we are forced to

149

artificially reintroduce them, people turn to methods of cooking that our earliest ancestors understood well. Wholemeal bread, macrobiotics, tassajara – even real ale.

There's a balance here which has more than a passing resemblance to that which exists in the world of animals and which has been called the principle of 'homeostasis'. When times are hard, animals are forced to spread out and to limit their birth-rate so that the ratio of animals to natural resources remain roughly constant. When you see flocks of birds sitting on telegraph wires chirping away they are probably doing so in order to gauge the density of their numbers in a particular habitat. Too many birds means too little to eat and steps will be taken to correct this state of affairs. The system, by and large, works well. Man, however, has a tougher time because he has to engineer new social changes in order to achieve the same effect. When populations begin to increase at a dangerous rate he has to invent and encourage contraception, permit homosexuality and so on. This in turn, however, creates the need for further changes. Women, for example, are no longer tied to the home by constant child-rearing. They demand opportunities which previously would have been inappropriate. Further social changes result and new problems arise requiring yet more solutions.

And so, man is constantly caught up in the need for social change. He can't stand still because his ever-increasing powers result in increasingly radical shifts in his pattern of life. At the same time he remains trapped by the same basic constraints which face all men and indeed all animals. Whatever his solutions, they are solutions of problems which are timeless. He can only add to, but not subtract from these.

Aggro has always supplied the solution to aggression. We've made life very difficult for ourselves and we've produced situations where death and destruction are inevitable. We've added to the problems of our own aggressiveness by building unnaturally large social units within which management of this force is extremely difficult. But, just as we return to brown bread and solar panels, it is not inconceivable that we might also return to the patterns of conflict resolution that the Dani find so easy to live with.

On the football terraces, fans have discovered just one way of being tribal. They don't live in tribes. In fact the housing estates on which many live are about as far removed from the image of a community as you can get. But on Saturdays things are different. The same is true in the Roxy Club or the Vortex in Wardour Street. By being a Punk, by dressing up and talking and dancing in a particular way, you can become a member of a highly distinctive

150

tribe. People don't want to identify with the whole of the human race – the 'Family of Man' is a misguided notion. They want to identify with a group which is a true social unit. That unit may be nested within a larger subculture, like that of New Wave or the soccer terraces in general – that's what provides the sense of being part of something that's 'bigger than yourself'. But it's the close bonding within the immediate sub-units which provides for the possibility of real social identity and restraint. Like the Dani warrior, fans and punks can fight because their fights can be limited and kept within safe boundaries through immediate and meaningful social conventions and constraints.

The more such tribe-like groups are established the less we are likely to see the trend towards violence which emerges out of depersonalization and alienation from a way of living that has its roots in the world of nature. And as societies become increasingly concerned with the more general aspects of tribal traditions and values, the less we are impelled towards the holocausts which follow in the wake of their neglect. The hippie teaches us a lesson in ecological and social management. And the bovver boy teaches us a lesson in the management of aggression. The lessons are not spelled out in what they say. The hippie talks metaphysically of flower-power and loving the entire world, and the bovver boy talks of kicking shit out of the guys down the road. None of this sounds promising. But the lesson is told in what they do. They teach by example not by rhetoric. And it's our eyes rather than our ears which have to be opened if we are to understand the message. We have to put aside our gross stereotypes and false images and begin to look at what is actually happening all around us.

The solution to the problem of violence lies within our grasp. We can't all live in tribes any more – we've gone well past the point where that is a reasonable possibility. But we can be alert to the values and cultural forces which were once securely rooted in the community – in the natural units in which we once had no choice but to live. As we slowly wake up to our predicament, fixed ideas of progress and notions of the automated paradise begin to seem less realistic. Something is found to be lacking in the dream. We feel compelled to reach back and retrieve some of the things we once felt happy to leave behind. In doing so, the restoration of balance begins, and the cultural see-saw starts, marginally, to level.

This guarded optimism here should not be confused with complacency – that's something we really can't afford. People such as authors and journalists who work to fixed deadlines often remark that their work usually gets done on time despite frequent set-backs and problems. But they only achieve this by constantly worrying and fearing that things won't work out at all. In a similar way, the world doesn't change itself. It changes because people are so moved by a fear of the future that they create an alternative future. As men and women react to the conditions around them, and as the defects within their patterns of life become manifestly obvious, a clearer picture emerges of what the alternatives might be, and what will be needed to achieve them. We are forced to choose, however, between futures which are realistic and those which are merely Utopian speculations. And even then we have to fret like hell that we might be wrong despite the fact that all the evidence suggests we are right.

Some proposed solutions, of course, can be discarded without hesitation. In particular, we can rid ourselves of some of the fanciful ideas which develop as a result of watching too many movies. In *Rollerball* and *Death Race 2000* people flock to sporting events where others die because it's in the rules of the game that they should. By watching such carnage everybody goes home happy and folk no longer feel the urge to beat their wives or fight with their neighbours. But whilst Hollywood directors may have vivid imaginations they are exceptionally poor guides to reality. Watching violence can have a number of effects. It can make some individuals feel a bit more aggressive but it can make others less so. In others it depends on the context and mood in which it is watched and for many, watching violence has no discernible effect at all. The overall effect on a society is, at best, unpredictable and, at worst, potentially harmful.

Not only are such ideas as these rather dangerous, they also miss the fundamental point that the expression of aggression is an active process. Whatever is provided in the way of vicarious experience, people will continue to seek out opportunities for forcibly putting down rivals, establishing special identities and carving out reputations. And it's with the availability of these opportunities that we must be concerned. In particular, we have to be alert to the fact that appropriate opportunities are required. Aggro always reflects, in the precise form that it takes, the needs, values and aspirations of particular groups of people. The principles are always the same but the social rituals and ceremonies vary in the light of the wider cultural framework within which they are situated.

I suggested at the beginning of this book that many of us don't need the soccer terraces, street corners or beer cellars because we have other opportunities readily available to us in our everyday lives. Because we live in societies which attach great importance to linguistic and academic abilities we can achieve our identities and reputations quite easily and work out our aggression through pursuits which meet with almost unanimous approval. We might, for example, turn to the game of chess as an opportunity for conflict. Some would say that chess is a passive exercise in pure logic and intense concentration. But the point of the game is to beat your rival – to symbolically kill his army and his clergy and capture his monarchy. The game, in fact, is the ultimate in socialized warfare. But it only works as a form of aggro within social contexts where skill at the game is considered meritorious. Outside of these contexts it is completely ineffective. You can't subdue an Arsenal fan, for example, by chanting out the fact that his endgame is lousy.

We are forced to the conclusion that whatever kind of society we construct, we can never come up with a single means of expressing aggression. Different people and different groups of people demand different social arenas and their own distinctive rituals. And the idea that we might produce a whole world in which board games were the basis of universal aggro is a very suspect notion. We shouldn't be seeking to impose blueprints like this at all. Instead our future is to be found in letting the more spontaneous and natural frameworks for aggression emerge as relevant and meaningful for those who participate within them. We can't institutionalize aggro, in the same way that we can't institutionalize tribes. What we can do, however, is provide a social backdrop which doesn't interfere with them to the extent that their useful function is negated. Instead of more external controls on aggressive behaviour, we need less. For as external controls increase there is always a corresponding decrease in internal controls, in the subtle social constraints which keep aggression in check. The bovver boys only keep their bundles in order when they feel themselves responsible for what goes on within their groups. Once that responsibility is eroded, trouble begins.

So the alternative future involves no sensational gimmick, nor a bizarre revolution in our life-styles. It involves simply a slow but sure retreat from some of the follies we have created in a short span of history. It involves recognition of basic human requirements and processes and a better understanding of what human nature is really all about. There's no rosy paradise to retreat to, no new Jerusalem around the corner. We're saddled with much the same fundamental processes as other primates. And no matter what we may achieve in the way of sophisticated cultural development, we have to remember that fact. Man is a social animal. But he is *by nature* a social animal. He builds upon foundations which are a legacy of his evolutionary roots. Our future lies not in a futile attempt to cut ourselves off from these roots but in social progress which proceeds in harmony with them. We have the potential to become at least as successful as the chimp in turning our conflicts into rituals. And by learning to live with aggro again we take a step in the right direction. We begin to see that illusions of violence are much preferable to the very real violence which maims and kills. Stylized bundles between rival gangs are far easier to cope with than gratuitous muggings. The survival of our societies has a price. And aggro, along with the retrieval of essential tribal values, is part of this price. When faced with the prospect of sudden extinction, the cost looks very small.

Bibliographical Notes

The following works represent a cross-section of the major source material used in the preparation of this book. Some of the books and articles are mentioned in the text, but others are given as a guide to further reading or acknowledgment of more diffuse influences. The more esoteric and technical works, many of which are unobtainable outside of university libraries, have been omitted. However, some of the books listed below contain extensive bibliographies which include such material and the most useful ones are indicated by an asterisk.

GENERAL
* T. Maple and D. W. Matheson, *Aggression, Hostility and Violence: Nature or Nurture* (New York, 1973).
* H. Toch, *Violent Men* (Harmondsworth, 1972).
* A. Storr, *Human Aggression* (Harmondsworth, 1968).
* J. P. Scott, *Aggression* (Chicago, 1958).
D. Morris, *The Naked Ape* (London, 1967).
D. Morris, *The Human Zoo* (London, 1969).
* K. Lorenz, *On Aggression* (London, 1966).
R. Leakey and R. Lewin, *Origins* (London, 1977).
* A. Montagu, *The Nature of Human Aggression* (New York and Oxford, 1976).
R. Hinde, 'The Nature of Aggression', *New Society* (9), 2nd March 1967.
* I. Eibl-Eibesfeldt, *Love and Hate* (London, 1971).

CHAPTER 1
A lot has been written on the subject of 'football hooliganism' in the last few years. Much of this material, however, is directed towards 'solutions' to the 'problem' rather than to understanding of the phenomenon. The Government's white papers on the subject are

amongst the worst offenders in this respect. More realistic accounts, however, are to be found in the following.
J. Clarke, 'Football Hooliganism and the Skinheads' and C. Crichter, 'Football and Cultural Values', occasional papers – Centre for Contemporary Cultural Studies, University of Birmingham.
* R. Ingham (ed.), *Football Hooliganism: The Wider Context* (Inter-Action Inprint, 1978).
I. Taylor, 'Hooligans: Soccer's Resistance Movement', *New Society,* 7th Aug. 1969.
I. Taylor, 'Football Mad' in E. Dunning (ed.), *The Sociology of Sport* (London, 1970).

My own research work is written up in more detail in:
P. Marsh, E. Rosser and R. Harré, *The Rules of Disorder* (London, 1978).
P. Marsh, 'Life and Careers on the Soccer Terraces' in R. Ingham (ed.), *Football Hooliganism – The Wider Context* (Inter-Action Inprint, 1978).
The topic of insult and obscene gestures is dealt with in Desmond Morris, *Manwatching* (London, 1977); and in D. Morris, P. Collett, P. Marsh and M. O'Shaughnessy, *Gesture Maps* (London, 1978).
An interesting analysis of some aspects of verbal abuse is to be found in Edmund Leach, 'Anthropological Aspects of Language: Animal Categories and Verbal Abuse' in E. H. Lenneberg (ed.), *New Directions in the Study of Language* (Boston, 1964).

CHAPTER 2
The main works referred to in this chapter are:
* Roger Johnson, *Aggression in Man and Animals* (Philadelphia, 1972).
* Ashley Montagu, *The Nature of Human Aggression* (New York and Oxford, 1976).
Konrad Lorenz, 'Ritual Fighting' in T. Maple & D. W. Matheson (eds.), *Aggression, Hostility and Violence: Nature or Nurture* (New York, 1973).
Desmond Morris, *The Naked Ape* (London, 1967).
Jane Van Lawick-Goodall 'Chimpanzees of the Gombe Stream Reserve' in I. De Vore (ed.), *Primate Behaviour* (New York, 1965).
Jan van Hooff, 'A structural analysis of the social behaviour of a semi-captive group of chimpanzees' in M. von Cranach and I. Vine (eds.), *Expressive Movement & Non-Verbal Communication* (London, 1972).
I. Eibl-Eibesfeldt, *Love and Hate* (London, 1971).

Sir Julian Huxley, 'Ritualisation of Behaviour in Animals and Man', *Proceedings of the Royal Zoological Society,* Series B, 1969.
N. Tinbergen, 'On War and Peace in Animals and Man', *Science,* vol. 160, 1968.

Further detailed accounts of aggression in animals can be found in:
N. Tinbergen, 'On War and Peace in Animals and Man', *Science,* vol. 160, 1968.
* I. De Vore, *Primate Behaviour* (New York, 1965).
* J. D. Carthy and F. J. Ebling (eds.), *The Natural History of Aggression* (London, 1964).

CHAPTER 3
Main references:
R. Gardner and K. Heider, *The Gardens of War* (Harmondsworth, 1974).
M. Harris, *Cows, Pigs, Wars and Witches* (London, 1974).
N. Chagnon, *Yanamamö – The Fierce People* (2nd Edition, New York, 1977).
R. Fox, *Encounter With Anthropology* (New York, 1973).

CHAPTER 4
Main references:
Pliny (the Younger), *Letters,* Book IX, 6 (Oxford, 1963).
* A. Cameron, *Circus Factions: Blues and Greens at Rome and Byzantium* (Oxford, 1976).
R. Fox, 'The Inherent Rules of Violence' in P. Collett (ed.), *Social Rules and Social Behaviour* (Oxford, 1976).
M. Howard, *War in European History* (Oxford, 1976).
H. Knipe and G. Maclay, *The Dominant Man* (London, 1972).
R. Baldick, *The Duel* (London, 1965).
Joe Frantz, 'The Frontier Tradition: An Invitation to Violence' in H. D. Graham and T. R. Gurr (eds.), *The History of Violence in America* (New York, 1969).
William FitzStephen, *Descriptio Nobilissimae Civitatis Londinae* (1175). (Quoted in P. Young, *A History of British Football* (London, 1968).)
Phillip Stubbes, *The Anatomy of Abuses* (1583).
N. Elias and E. Dunning, 'Folk Football in Medieval and Early Modern Britain' in E. Dunning (ed.), *The Sociology of Sport* (London, 1970).
N. Cohn, *A WopBopaLooBopLopBamBoom* (London, 1970).
S. Cohen, *Folk Devils and Moral Panics* (London, 1973).

Bibliographical Notes

CHAPTER 5
Main references:
R. Ardrey, *The Territorial Imperative* (London, 1969).
A. Montagu, *The Nature of Human Aggression* (New York and Oxford, 1976).
* Louis Yablonsky, *The Violent Gang* (New York, 1962).
O. Newman, *Defensible Space* (London, 1969).
D. Morris, *The Naked Ape* (London, 1967).
F. M. Thrasher, *The Gang* (Chicago, 1936).
Other useful books in this area are:
J. Patrick, *A Glasgow Gang Observed* (London, 1970).
R. Sommer, *Personal Space* (Englewood Cliffs, N.J., 1969).

CHAPTER 6
Main references:
R. Ardrey, *African Genesis* (New York, 1961).
R. Ardrey, *The Territorial Imperative* (London, 1969).
R. Ardrey, *The Hunting Hypothesis* (London, 1976).
G. Reitlinger, *The Final Solution* (London, 1953).
* H. Kelman, 'Violence Without Moral Restraint', *Journal of Social Issues,* vol. 29, 1973.
S. Milgram, 'Conditioning of Obedience and Disobedience to Authority', *International Journal of Psychiatry,* vol. 6, 1968.
L. Tiger and R. Fox, *The Imperial Animal* (New York, 1971).
L. Tiger, *Men in Groups* (Sunbury-on-Thames, 1969).
C. Taylor, *The Warriors of the Plains* (London, 1975).

CHAPTER 7
Main references:
J. Herbers, Special Introduction in H. D. Graham and T. R. Gurr (eds.), *The History of Violence in America* (New York, 1969).
T. Gurr, Introduction to H. D. Graham and T. R. Gurr (eds.), *Violence in America: Historical and Comparative Perpectives* (U.S. Government Printing Office, 1969).
J. Rowbottom, 'A History of Violence' in N. Tutt (ed.) *Violence* (HMSO, 1976).
G. Pearson, 'In Defence of Hooliganism' in N. Tutt (ed.), *Violence* (HMSO, 1976).
J. Q. Wilson, 'Crime in the Streets' in S. Endleman (ed.), *Violence in the Streets* (Chicago, 1968).
R. Fox, *Encounter With Anthropology* (New York, 1973).
R. Fox, 'The Inherent Rules of Violence' in P. Collett (ed.), *Social Rules and Social Behaviour* (Oxford, 1976).

E. Thomas, *The Harmless People* (New York, 1959).

R. Lee, '! Kung Bushmen Violence' (paper presented to American Anthropological Association, New Orleans, 1969).

A. Montagu, *The Nature of Human Aggression* (Oxford, 1976).

B. Bettelheim, 'Violence: A Neglected Mode of Behaviour' in S. Endelman (ed.), *Violence in the Streets* (Chicago, 1968).

* J. Goldstein, *Aggression and Crimes of Violence* (New York and Oxford, 1975).

M. Hunt, *The Mugging* (Harmondsworth, 1976).

Index

Index

Index

164